Routledge
Taylor & Francis Group

LONDON AND NEW YORK

Eighth edition published 2012
by Routledge
2 Park Square, Milton Park, Abingdon, Oxon OX14 4RN

Simultaneously published in the USA and Canada
by Routledge
711 Third Avenue, New York, NY 10017

Routledge is an imprint of the Taylor & Francis Group, an informa business

First edition published by Cavendish Publishing Limited 1997
Seventh edition published by Routledge 2010

British Library Cataloguing in Publication Data
A catalogue record for this book is available from the British Library

ISBN: 978-0-415-68334-0 (pbk)
ISBN: 978-0-203-29880-0 (ebk)

Typeset in Rotis
by RefineCatch Limited, Bungay, Suffolk

Printed and bound in Great Britain by
TJ International Ltd, Padstow, Cornwall

Contents

Table of Cases

Table of Statutes

Table of Statutory Instruments

Table of European Legislation

How to use this book

Welcome to this new edition of Routledge-Cavendish English Legal System Lawcards. In response to student feedback, we've added some new features to these new editions to give you all the support and preparation you need in order to face your law exams with confidence.

Inside this book you will find:

▓ NEW tables of cases and statutes for ease of reference

■ Revision Checklists

We've summarised the key topics you will need to know for your law exams and broken them down into a handy revision checklist. Check them out at the beginning of each chapter, then after you have the chapter down, revisit the checklist and tick each topic off as you gain knowledge and confidence.

1

Sources of law

Primary legislation: Acts of Parliament	■
Secondary legislation	■
Case law	■
System of precedent	■
Common law	■
Equity	■
EU law	■
Human Rights Act 1998	■

■ Key Cases

We've identified the key cases that are most likely to come up in exams. To help you to ensure that you can cite cases with ease, we've included a brief account of the case and judgment for a quick aide-memoire.

HENDY LENNOX v GRAHAME PUTTICK [1984]

Basic facts

Diesel engines were supplied, subject to a *Romalpa* clause, then fitted to generators. Each engine had a serial number. When the buyer became insolvent the seller sought to recover one engine. The Receiver argued that the process of fitting the engine to the generator passed property to the buyer. The court disagreed and allowed the seller to recover the still identifiable engine despite the fact that some hours of work would be required to disconnect it.

Relevance

If the property remains identifiable and is not irredeemably changed by the manufacturing process a *Romalpa* clause may be viable.

■ Companion Website

At the end of each chapter you will be prompted to visit the Routledge-Cavendish Lawcards companion website where you can test your understanding online with specially prepared multiple choice questions, as well as revise the key terms with our online glossary.

You should now be confident that you would be able to tick all of the boxes on the checklist at the beginning of this chapter. To check your knowledge of Sources of law why not visit the companion website and take the Multiple Choice Question test. Check your understanding of the terms and vocabulary used in this chapter with the flashcard glossary.

Exam Practice

Once you've acquired the basic knowledge, you'll want to put it to the test. The Routledge-Cavendish Questions and Answers provides examples of the kinds of questions that you will face in your exams, together with suggested answer plans and a fully-worked model answer. We've included one example free at the end of this book to help you put your technique and understanding into practice.

QUESTION 1

What are the main sources of law today?

Answer plan

This is, apparently, a very straightforward question, but the temptation is to ignore the European Community (EU) as a source of law and to over-emphasise custom as a source. The following structure does not make these mistakes:

- in the contemporary situation, it would not be improper to start with the EU as a source of UK law;

- then attention should be moved on to domestic sources of law: statute and common law;

- the increased use of delegated legislation should be emphasised;

- custom should be referred to, but its extremely limited operation must be emphasised.

ANSWER

European law

Since the UK joined the European Economic Community (EEC), now the EU, it has progressively but effectively passed the power to create laws which are operative in this country to the wider European institutions. The UK is now subject to Community law, not just as a direct consequence of the various treaties of accession passed by the UK Parliament, but increasingly, it is subject to the secondary legislation generated by the various institutions of the EU.

The contract of employment

The distinction between employees and independent contractors in employment status

The evolution of the tests at common law

Application of the three-stage test established in *Ready Mixed Concrete (South East) Ltd v Minister of Pensions and National Insurance* [1968]

Understanding and application of the 'business on own account' test for employment status

Appreciation of the significance of 'mutuality of obligations' in determining 'employee' status

The limitations of the parties' use of labels in determining employment status

The sources of the contract of employment

The major provisions required under s 1 Employment Rights Act 1996, known as the 'written particulars'

The implied terms that provide rights and obligations for the employer and the employee

The protections a restraint of trade clause provides to an employer when an employee leaves the business

The protection of a worker's health and safety through the Working Time Regulations 1998

EMPLOYED OR SELF-EMPLOYED?

The difference between an employee and a self-employed person is of crucial importance for a number of reasons. Only employees qualify for:

- social security payments, such as jobseeker's allowance, statutory sick pay, etc;

- employment protection rights, such as unfair dismissal, redundancy payments, minimum notice on termination, etc;

- rights under the Equality Act 2010; Pt II of the Employment Rights Act (ERA) 1996 (unlawful deductions from wages); and the Disability Discrimination Act 1995 are significant exceptions – their coverage extends beyond employees to individuals who personally perform the task. Generally speaking, EC law applies to 'workers', a broader term than 'employees';

- certain health and safety provisions;

- the benefit of the employer's duty of care at common law to protect employees (such as the vicarious liability of the employer) (see *Lane v Shire Roofing Co (Oxford) Ltd* [1995]);

- taxation under Schedule E to the Income and Corporation Taxes Act 1988, and tax is deducted under the PAYE system, whereas a self-employed person is liable to tax under Schedule D, with its more generous allowances.

The terminology is as follows: an employee is employed under a 'contract **of** employment' (or of service), whereas a self-employed person (independent contractor) works under a 'contract **for** services'. Under s 230(3) of ERA 1996, a worker (a broader term used in legislation such as the Working Time Regulations 1998), is defined as an individual who has entered into, or works under (or, where the employment has creased, worked under) a contract of employment or any other contract whereby the individual undertakes to perform personally any work or services for another party to the contract whose status is not a client or customer of any profession or business undertaking carried on by the individual. Hence, those who undertake work personally may be held as workers for the purposes of protective statutory rights.

A STATUTORY DEFINITION

Section 230(1) of the ERA 1996 defines an employee as 'an individual who has entered into or works under a contract of service'. This definition is deliberately broad due to the difficulties in establishing a single test to cover the wide range of jobs in the modern era; if a test is provided by statute this would allow employers greater scope to affect the employment status of their workers and hence avoid certain rights and obligations; and statutes are rigid and not as easily updated in light of developments in the workplace or society as is case law. Therefore, for an accurate assessment of determining employment status, reference has to be made to the case law:

STATUTORY INTERPRETATION BY CASE LAW

A number of tests have emerged over a period of time:

- The 'control' test: *Yewens v Noakes* [1880].

▶ YEWENS v NOAKES [1880]

Control continues to be a vital element in the assessment of employment status, however it is not to be used in isolation.

The case involved an employer who had allowed a worker to reside in a suite of premises owned by him. It was important to determine the worker's status as if the worker was held to be a servant (now an employee) the employer would have avoided a tax on the property; if the worker was an independent contractor, the tax would be levied.

It was held that the control exercisable by the employer was crucial to determining the worker's employee status.

- The control test was modified to the 'right to control' and applied in *Walker v Crystal Palace Football Club* [1910].

▶ WALKER v THE CRYSTAL PALACE FOOTBALL CLUB LIMITED [1910]

This case involved a professional footballer, who was injured in a match and was consequently unable to play again.

At the end of the one-year agreement, the club refused to renew his contract and he required employee status in order to qualify for a claim under insurance. Here the 'control' test was modified in light of an increasingly skilled workforce, and therefore this case established the employer's 'right to control' (i.e. hours of work; place of work and so on) was the determining factor.

▣ The 'integration' test: *Stevenson, Jordan and Harrison v MacDonald and Evans* [1952].

> ❱ STEVENSON, JORDAN AND HARRISON v MACDONALD AND EVANS [1952]

This case involved a former manager at a company who, following retirement, wrote a book based on a series of lectures given, in part, whilst employed at the company and based on research funded by it. When the text was sent to the publishers, the company wished to stop publication until it was decided who owned the intellectual property rights to the content – the author or the company.

To answer this question the test of 'integration' into the organisation was developed. The more integrated the individual was in the workforce, the more likely he was to be held an employee. The closer he was to the periphery, the more likely he was to be held an independent contractor. However, as Denning LJ did not define what 'integrated' meant, this was a little used test.

▣ The 'mixed'/'multiple'/'economic reality' test: *Ready Mixed Concrete v Ministry of Pensions* [1968].

> ❱ READY MIXED CONCRETE (SOUTH EAST) LTD v MINISTER OF PENSIONS AND NATIONAL INSURANCE [1968]

This case involved a series of 'owner-drivers' who were in the business of delivering concrete products for the company. In a question between the company and the government department over the correct status of the drivers, the following three-stage questions should be applied: (1) Does the worker agree to provide his skill in consideration of a wage; (2) Is there a degree of control exercisable by the employer; and (3) Are there other provisions of the contract which are inconsistent with a contract of service.

In this case, the drivers were independent contractors as they could hire other drivers and they could own more than one vehicle in the firm.

▪ The 'business on own account' test in *Market Investigations v Ministry of Social Security* [1969].

▶ MARKET INVESTIGATIONS LTD v MINISTRY OF SOCIAL SECURITY [1969]

The case involved a number of interviewers working for a market research company. The firm employed a small number of full-time interviewers and relied mainly on the services of casual interviewers. The case demonstrated that whilst these workers were employed only for short periods of time (the length of each interview), each of these created a series of contracts and thereby a 'global' or 'umbrella' contract.

The key element of the employment status is whether the individual is in business on his/her own account. If yes, then he/she is an independent contractor, if not then he/she is an employee.

It is important to note that in cases such as *Hall (HM Inspector of Taxes) v Lorimer* [1994] the courts have taken a more overall or 'holistic' view of the situation, and warned against the strict (or mechanical) application of the tests developed in the cases above.

Sources and terms of the contract of employment

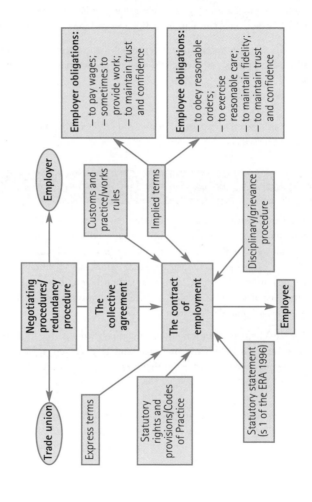

> ▶ HALL (HM INSPECTOR OF TAXES) v LORIMER [1994]

Mr Lorimer left his previous position in full-time employment and became a freelance vision mixer to benefit, in part, from better tax provisions. He worked for a number of companies, but his engagements were of a short-term basis (the longest was for 10 days). When he was dismissed, he attempted to revert back to employee status to gain protection from the unfair dismissal legislation.

The Court of Appeal concurred with Mummery J. in the High Court, that the tests to establish employment status should not be part of a 'mechanical exercise.' Instead, all the factors of the employment should be considered as not all the details of the facts are of equal importance.

In determining employment status, the modern approach has been to adopt a multi-factorial test, weighing up the various factors for and against the existence of a contract of employment. *Ready Mixed Concrete v Ministry of Pensions* [1968] lays down a three-stage test (which was impliedly approved by the House of Lords in *Carmichael plc v National Power* [2000]):

■ the worker agrees to provide his work in return for a wage;

■ the worker agrees to be subject to the control of the other party; and

■ the other provisions of the contract are consistent with it being a contract of employment

Montgomery v Johnson Underwood Ltd [2001] may be considered the major authority and states that there must be mutuality of obligation between the parties, as evidenced by the existence of a contract, and there must exist a sufficiency of control by the 'employer' over the individual – only if both of these conditions are satisfied should a tribunal go on to find that a contract of employment exists (see *O'Kelly and Others v Trusthouse Forte* [1983]). The Employment Appeal Tribunal (EAT) in *Knight v BCCP Ltd* [2011] recently reaffirmed the essential feature of mutuality of obligations to establish an employment relationship for the purposes of Employment Rights Act 1996.

> ### ▶ MONTGOMERY v JOHNSON UNDERWOOD LTD [2001]
>
> In the case of an agency worker it had to be determined if she was employed by the agency, the company worked for, or if she was not an employee in any sense. It was held that two elements are crucial in identifying a worker with 'employee' status – control and mutuality of obligations.
>
> There must be an element of control exercisable by the employer, and mutuality of obligations between the parties. Only if these two questions are answered in the affirmative should the tribunal continue to determine employment status.

In the case of work which is part time, casual or otherwise 'atypical', the case law is at times confusing. The current position is best defined by *Carmichael v National Power plc* [2000] (HL), as applied in such cases as *Montgomery v Johnson Underwood Ltd* [2001]. This means the tribunal will determine the issues by looking at the reality of the employment situation, rather than applying a legal test.

In relation to agency workers, specific and clear guidance on the previous case law and how to determine employment status was provided by the EAT in *James v Greenwich LBC* [2008]. Later the Court of Appeal held such employment could only be with the agency, rather than the employer worked for. Note that from 1st October 2011, the Agency Workers Regulations 2010 will come into force. These Regulations provide agency workers (hence persons engaged on a temporary basis) with the same rights as provided to permanent workers in respect of basic working and employment conditions (pay, holidays, etc). These rights become effective where the agency worker has been engaged for 12 consecutive weeks or longer.

The tribunal and courts assess the importance of the factors that either point towards or away from a contract of employment in each case. However, an important factor to determine employee status is that contracts of employment are contracts of 'personal service'. Consequently, a term in the contract that the individual need not personally do the job is a strong indicator that he/she is self-employed: *Express and Echo Publications Ltd v Tanton* [1999] and *MacFarlane v Glasgow CC* [2001]. The EAT in *Community Dental Centres Ltd v Sultan-Darmon* [2010] held that an unfettered right to provide substitutes (hence where the work did not need to be performed personally) was fatal to the status as a 'worker', not simply 'employee' status.

A question of law or fact?

Whether a contract is a contract of employment or a contract for services has been clearly stated to be a question of fact, unless the sole issue is the construction of documents. As such, it is a matter for the employment tribunal, as long as it directs itself properly as to the legal tests to be applied (see *McLeod v Hellyer Bros Ltd* [1987]; *Lee v Chung and Shun Shing Construction & Engineering Co Ltd* [1990]; cf *Davies v Presbyterian Church of Wales* [1986]). A 'question of fact' regarding mutuality of obligations between the parties was recently demonstrated in *Breakell v Shropshire Army Cadet Force* [2010]. Here the EAT confirmed that a tribunal's assessment of the (non)-existence of mutuality of obligations could be based on a factual assessment.

Self-description

The fact that the parties have labelled the relationship as one of self-employment is not viewed as a decisive factor by the tribunals; it is merely one factor to be considered (see *Ferguson v John Dawson & Partners Ltd* [1976]; *Young and Woods Ltd v West* [1980]; *Lane v Shire Roofing Co (Oxford) Ltd* [1995]; cf *Massey v Crown Life Insurance Co* [1978]).

> ### ❯ LANE v THE SHIRE ROOFING COMPANY (OXFORD) LTD [1995]
>
> This case involved a self-employed builder who began employment with the defendants as an independent contractor. Mr Lane was injured when he undertook a roofing job as he used his own ladders instead of the appropriate scaffold. The defendants accepted they had responsibility for the health and safety of the worker.
>
> It was held that if, as in this case, the employer is deliberately attempting to use the status of the worker to avoid providing adequate health and safety protection to an individual, the tribunals will hold the individual as an 'employee' to prevent the employer circumventing the law.

The tribunals will be guided by the label used in the contract, but will endeavour to identify the true nature of the employment relationship.

> ▶ FERGUSON v JOHN DAWSON & PARTNERS (CONTRACTORS)
> LTD [1976]
>
> The case concerned a builder who had been engaged to work 'on
> the lump' with no tax or national insurance deducted from the pay
> he received. The employer had defined the builder's employment
> status as that of an independent contractor, but in reality he worked
> under the control of the foreman and was provided with the tools
> to perform the job.
>
> The Court of Appeal held him to be an employee. This was due to
> an examination of the nature of the employment, and holding that
> the label attached to the builder was merely persuasive and not
> conclusive.

Ministers of religion

The EAT in *Moore v The President of the Methodist Conference* [2010] held that
a Minister of the Methodist Church, and appointed as Superintendent Minister
on a Methodist Church Circuit, is an employee of the Church and thus entitled
to protection under unfair dismissal legislation. This principle was further
established by the Court of Appeal in *Maga v Trustees of the Birmingham
Archdiocese of the Roman Catholic Church* [2010] regarding employee status
and the vicarious liability of the Roman Catholic Church.

THE INDIVIDUAL CONTRACT AND ITS SOURCES

Features:

- inequality of bargaining power;

- informality.

Sources:

- express terms;

- collective bargaining;

- implied terms;

- work rules;

- custom and practice;

- statute;

- awards under statutory provisions.

Contracts of employment have been subject to the general rules of contract. All the normal contractual rules, such as offer, acceptance, consideration and legality, apply to the contract of employment. As the bargaining powers of the two parties are in most situations unequal, statutory measures have been incorporated to provide a minimum of protection.

Statute provides for the protection of employees in the termination of the employment contract, implies terms, including the written particulars of employment, and regulates against discrimination.

In many situations, a physical contract of employment is not provided (particularly by employers with few employees). Only in exceptional cases must the contract itself be in writing, for example, cases involving the Merchant Shipping Act 1995 and contracts of apprenticeship.

The contract of employment includes express and implied terms of which it is important to be aware. Examples of terms implied into the contract are included below, and examples of express terms include covenants in restraint of trade.

EMPLOYMENT PARTICULARS

Most employees possess the right to receive a written statement of some of the most important terms of the contract of employment, not later than two months after entering employment (see s 1 of the ERA 1996). Changes must be notified to employees individually, at the latest, not more than one month after the change.

The statement may be given in instalments during the two-month period (s 1 of the ERA 1996). However, certain particulars must be contained in a single document. These are the names of the parties; the dates when employment and continuous employment commenced; the particulars of remuneration; hours and holidays; the job title or description; and the place of work (s 2(4) of the ERA 1996).

Particulars that must be supplied

The written statement must specify:

- the names of the employer and the employee (s 3(a));

- the date that the employment began (s 3(b));

- the date that the employee's period of continuous employment began (taking into account any employment with a previous employer which counts towards that period) (s 3(c));

- the scale or rate of remuneration, or the method of calculating remuneration (s 4(a));

- the intervals at which remuneration is paid (s 4(b));

- any terms and conditions relating to hours of work (including any terms and conditions relating to normal working hours) (s 4(c));

- any terms and conditions relating to:

  - entitlement to holidays, including public holidays and holiday pay (s 4(d)(i));

  - incapacity to work due to sickness or injury, including any provisions for sick pay (s 4(d)(ii));

  - pension and pension schemes (s 4(d)(iii));

- the length of notice which the employee is obliged to give and entitled to receive in order to terminate the contract of employment (s 4(e));

- the title of the job which the employee is employed to do or a brief description of the work for which the employee is employed (s 4(f));

- where the employment is not intended to be permanent, the period for which it is expected to continue or, if it is for a fixed term, the date on which it is to end (s 4(g));

- either the place of work or, if the employee is required or permitted to work at various places, an indication of that and the employer's address (s 4(h));

- any collective agreements which directly affect the terms and conditions of employment, including the persons by whom they were made where the employer is not a party (s 4(j));

■ where the employee is required to work outside the UK for more than a month, certain further particulars concerning that period, the currency of remuneration, any additional remuneration and benefits, and any terms and conditions relating to return (s 4(k)).

Significance of the particulars

These terms are essential evidence for many statutory-based claims that protect employees such as:

■ identifying the commencement of employment – unfair dismissal and redundancy have minimum periods of service before qualification is gained and the levels of compensation are calculated on the number of years in service;

■ the notice period required – relevant for wrongful dismissal claims (particularly in situations involving fixed-term contracts);

■ the sources of terms – such as works' handbooks and collective agreements;

■ payments for illness or absences from work.

In the absence of this document, and where the contract of employment has not been provided, establishing claims to rights or defining obligations is made much more time consuming and difficult.

The statement is not a contract in itself

Until 1982, it was thought that s 1 statements had virtually equivalent weight to a written contract, that is, they were affected by the parol evidence rule (see *Gascol Conversions v Mercer* [1974]).

However, since *System Floors v Daniel* [1982], the position is as follows:

It seems to us ... that, in general, the status of the statutory statement is this. It provides very strong *prima facie* evidence of what were the terms of the contract between the parties, but does not constitute a written contract between the parties. Nor are the statements of the terms finally conclusive: at most, they place a heavy burden on the employer to show that the actual terms of contract are different from those which he has set out in the statutory statement.

The contract of employment includes implied terms, in addition to these express terms, and it is for this reason, among others, that the employment particulars under s 1 of the ERA 1996 do not constitute the contract, even though many of the elements are included in both.

Remedies for failure to supply

See ss 11–12 of the ERA 1996 and *Eagland v British Telecom* [1992]. See also *Mears v Safecar Security Ltd* [1982], *Southern Cross Healthcare Co Ltd v Perkins and Others* [2010] and *Construction Industry Training Board v Leighton* [1978].

The Employment Act 2002, s 38 provides that in cases of unfair dismissal, redundancy or discrimination, if no written statement of employment particulars had been provided by the start of the proceedings, then a minimum of two weeks' wages, and a maximum of four weeks' wages (capped as of 1st February 2011 at £400 per week) is awarded.

THE PRODUCTS OF COLLECTIVE BARGAINING

Employers may find it easier to negotiate terms affecting employees with trades unions rather than negotiate contractual terms individually with each employee. As such, it is important to determine where these terms are included in a contract (through a works' handbook, staff intranet, human resources documents and so on), and which parties are bound by such provisions.

Collective agreements between employers and trade unions are not binding on those parties, but terms of the agreements may be incorporated into individual contracts of employment and so become legally binding between employers and their employees.

EFFECTS OF THE COLLECTIVE BARGAINING ON THE INDIVIDUAL CONTRACT OF EMPLOYMENT

There are three possible methods of incorporation:

- agency;
- express incorporation; and
- implied incorporation.

Agency

Although it is possible for a trade union to act as agent for its members, it would require express agreement to this effect from all parties.

See *Holland v London Society of Compositors* [1924]; *Burton Group Ltd v Smith* [1977]; cf *Singh v British Steel Corp* [1974]; *Land v West Yorkshire MCC* [1979].

Express incorporation

There are three problems:

■ What is the effect on the terms of an individual contract when an incorporated agreement is cancelled? See *Robertson v British Gas Corp* [1983]; *Gibbons v Associated British Ports* [1985], cf *Cadoux v Central Regional Council* [1986]; *Davies v Hotpoint Ltd* [1994].

■ Is the legal status of the source of the incorporated term important? See *Marley v Forward Trust Group* [1986].

■ The appropriateness question: see *Gallagher v Post Office* [1970]; *British Leyland UK Ltd v McQuilken* [1978]; *Alexander v Standard Telephone and Cables Ltd* [1991]; *City of Edinburgh Council v Brown* [1999]. A pay increase is the obvious example of a term that is suitable for incorporation into an individual employment contract.

Implied terms

Despite the increasing role played by statute (for example an equality clause imposed into all contracts of employment by the Equality Act 2010), common law implied terms are still of considerable importance. New terms can still be 'discovered'.

The traditional test for implication is objective and the courts will imply a term:

> . . . of which it can be predicated that it goes without saying; some term not expressed but necessary to give to the transaction such business efficacy as the parties must have intended [*Luxor Ltd v Cooper* [1941], *per* Lord Wright].

Is this test based on industrial reality?
There are two distinctive types of terms:

- those implied due to the particular circumstances of the case, often known as terms implied in fact;

- those implied due to the operation of the common law, often known as terms implied in law.

Factual implied terms

These terms are inserted into the contract of employment through the normal contractual tests, such as the business efficacy and 'officious bystander' tests. It was once thought that the correct approach was that of the usual objective rules, but an approach which comes nearer to that of implying terms where they would be reasonable has been adopted: see *Mears v Safecar Security Ltd* [1982]; *Jones v Associated Tunnelling Co Ltd* [1981]; *Courtaulds Northern Spinning Ltd v Sibson* [1988]; *Eagland v BT plc* [1992]. However, cf *Quinn v Calder Industrial Materials Ltd* [1996].

Terms implied by common law

Although many of these have evolved from the 19th century, there is no reason to suppose that this is a static area of law.

The employer's duties

There are generally thought to be the following implied duties on the part of the employer:

- to pay wages;

- to provide work (in certain circumstances);

- to provide a safe system of work;

- to maintain mutual trust and confidence;

- (exceptionally) to force a garden leave.

The employee's duties

The duties of the employee are generally thought to be:

- to obey lawful and reasonable orders;

- to adapt to new working practices;

- to exercise reasonable care and competence;

- to maintain fidelity (faithful service);

- not to compete with the employer whilst employed;

- not to misuse confidential information;

- not to impede the employer's business;

- to cooperate with the employer;

- to maintain mutual trust and confidence.

THE EMPLOYER'S DUTIES

Provide wages

Where the amount of wages or the frequency of the payments have not been agreed between the employee and employer there is an implied duty to pay wages (*Devonald v Rosser & Sons* [1906]).

The employer also has the duty to pay a fair proportion of wages if industrial action is accepted (*Miles v Wakefield MDC* [1987]).

The employer must pay wages in money (previous practices included paying in tokens redeemable in the employer's business).

> ▶ MILES v WAKEFIELD METROPOLITAN DISTRICT COUNCIL [1987]
>
> The superintendent registrar of births, deaths and marriages took industrial action by refusing to work on Saturday mornings
>
> Here the House of Lords held that the employer was entitled to withhold 3/37ths of his wages as Mr Miles was unavailable for work.

A right to work?

In general, the employer will not be in breach of contract by failing to provide work, as long as wages continue to be paid:

... Provided I pay my cook her wages regularly, she cannot complain if I choose to take any or all of my meals out (*Collier v Sunday Referee Publishing Co Ltd* [1940], *per* Asquith J).

Exceptions

There are exceptions to this general rule, including the following:

- where work depends wholly or partially on piecework payment or commission (see *Turner v Goldsmith* [1891]);

- where part of the consideration is publicity, for example, where an actor needs publicity in order to acquire his next role (see *Herbert Clayton and Jack Waller Ltd v Oliver* [1930]);

- where skills need to be maintained (such as surgeons) (see *Breach v Epsylon Industries Ltd* [1976]).

See also *Langston v AUEW* [1974].

Provide a safe system of work

Employers are under a twofold duty, namely, to provide a safe place of work; safe equipment and safe colleagues: *Wilsons & Clyde Coal Co Ltd v English* [1938]. For an interesting development, see *Johnstone v Bloomsbury HA* [1991]; *Cross v Highlands Enterprise* [2001]; *Spring v Guardian Assurance plc* [1993].

Mutual trust and confidence

The importance of this term has increased considerably over the past two decades: *Isle of Wight Tourist Board v Coombes* [1976]; *Woods v WM Car Services* [1981]; *Lewis v Motorworld Garages* [1986]; *Malik v Bank of Credit and Commerce International* [1997].

> ▶ ISLE OF WIGHT TOURIST BOARD v COOMBES [1976]
>
> The case involved the director of the Tourist Board who remarked to a colleague, following an argument with Coombes and in which she was present, that Coombes could be '... an intolerable bitch on a Monday morning'.
>
> It was held by the Employment Appeal Tribunal that this was demeaning and had breached the fundamental implied term of respect and confidence, thereby enabling the claimant to treat the breach as repudiatory and claim constructive dismissal.

THE EMPLOYEE'S DUTIES

Obedience to lawful and reasonable orders

With changing social attitudes, many of the earlier decisions upholding the employer's right to summarily dismiss employees for one act of disobedience would probably not be decided the same way today. See *Laws v London Chronicle Ltd* [1959]; *Wilson v Racher* [1974].

> ## ▶ WILSON v RACHER [1974]
>
> Wilson was a gardener of good character. Racher 'aggressively and provocatively' criticised him for refusing to use electric hedge cutters in the rain, and when Wilson attempted to walk away from the insults, he was subjected to even more abuse. As a result, Wilson used obscene language to Racher in front of Racher's wife and children and was summarily dismissed.
>
> It was held by the Court of Appeal that the dismissal was wrongful as the employer had started the action, and the employer's insistence that Wilson continue to use the cutters was not a lawful order as it could endanger the employee.

But compare with *Pepper v Webb* [1969].

> ## ▶ PEPPER v WEBB [1969]
>
> Here an employee was engaged as a gardener, whose work and attitude had recently diminished, and when asked to undertake some planting he responded 'I couldn't care less about your bloody greenhouse and your sodding garden'. He was summarily dismissed.
>
> The Court of Appeal agreed with the dismissal as this was a reasonable and lawful order, and the wilful disobedience was a fundamental breach of the contract.

Unreasonable/unlawful orders

The following have been held to be unreasonable orders:

▨ ordering an employee into immediate danger (*Ottoman Bank v Chakarian* [1930]);

▨ ordering an employee to commit an illegal act (*Morrish v Henlys (Folkestone) Ltd* [1973]).

Adapt to new working practices
As part of their managerial prerogative, the employer can adopt new working practices (such as using new technology and so on) and the employees have to adapt to using these. The employer must provide adequate training and time for the new skills to be developed. See *Cresswell v Board of Inland Revenue* [1984], *Hollister v NFU* [1979]. If the change involves altering the contractual terms, the employer can only lawfully introduce change if either:

▨ there is a term in the contract authorising fundamental variation; or

▨ the employee has agreed to the change: cf *Burdett-Coutts v Hertfordshire CC* [1984]; *Rigby v Ferodo* [1987]; *Security and Facilities v Hayes* [2001].

In *Bateman v Asda Stores Ltd* [2010], Asda sought to impose a new pay and conditions regime that sought to ensure all its staff worked under the same work and pay structure. Consequently, staff engaged on an older system had their contracts varied as a consequence of this business need. Asda claimed a right to take this action due to provisions in the staff handbook and, having carried out a full consultation with all the employees, varied the contracts accordingly. The affected staff who did not agree to the change brought an action for unauthorised deductions from their pay under s 13 ERA 1996. The EAT held that a broad contractual right to vary terms and conditions of employment may enable an employer's unilateral variation, even without the express consent of the affected employees. The changes, where properly implemented and where an employer acts to preserve the trust and confidence of the relationship, enabled Asda to harmonise the new pay structure adopted, even where a relatively small number of staff would not agree to the change.

Exercise reasonable care and competence
Employees must exercise reasonable skill and judgment in their employment so as not to endanger colleagues and clients.

Reasonable care includes a duty to maintain the health and safety of themselves and other workers: *Lister v Romford Ice & Cold Storage Co Ltd* [1957].

Competence in the execution of tasks at employment is a further duty, and a negligent act may lead to a breach of this implied term: *Janata Bank v Ahmed* [1981].

Maintain fidelity

This duty extends to obligations not to accept bribes, take secret profits or maintain the secrecy of one's colleagues' misdeeds, but it is in respect of competition that this duty is most often seen. In *Lonmar Global Risks Ltd v West and Others* [2010] the High Court held the requirement of disclosing to the employer an employee's own misdeed or that of fellow employees, rests where the employee is a fiduciary. A fiduciary duty was not established merely by the parties being involved in an employment relationship.

Not to compete with the employer whilst employed

See, in particular, the employee's obligations:

■ *Hivac Ltd v Park Royal Scientific Instruments Ltd* [1946];

■ *Smith v DuPont (UK) Ltd* [1976];

■ *Nova Plastics Ltd v Froggatt* [1982].

Competition: ex-employees

An ex-employee is generally free to go into competition with his/her former employer. This is subject to two exceptions.

(1) An employee may not do anything while still employed which is in breach of the duty of fidelity
See, for example, *Wessex Dairies Ltd v Smith* [1935]; *Robb v Green* [1895]; *Roger Bullivant Ltd v Ellis* [1987].

However, it is perfectly lawful for an ex-employee to canvass customers of his/ her former employer after leaving the service. Moreover, he/she is entitled to make use of the knowledge and skills acquired whilst in the former employer's business, apart from such information which can be classified as trade secrets. In this sense, the implied duty of confidentiality for ex-employees is narrower than in the case of an existing employee: see *Faccenda Chicken Ltd v Fowler* [1986].

▶ FACCENDA CHICKEN LTD v FOWLER [1986]

The company marketed fresh chickens and had employed Fowler as its sales manager. Fowler left the company to establish his own firm in the same area and recruited a number of Faccenda's staff. Faccenda applied for an injunction to stop Fowler from using the confidential sales information he had access to, even though there was no restraint of trade clause in his contract.

The request was refused. The Court of Appeal provided guidelines on whether any item of information falls within the implied term of confidentiality, so as to prevent its use or disclosure by an employee after employment has ceased.

The court will consider:

- the nature of the employment;

- the nature of the information, that is, whether it is a trade secret or some other highly confidential data;

- whether the employer impressed on the employee the confidentiality of the information;

- whether the relevant information can be isolated from other information which the employee is free to use or disclose.

See also *Lancashire Fires Ltd v SA Lyons* [1997]; *SBJ Stevenson Ltd v Mandy* [2000].

There is a defence of 'just cause or excuse' to an employee's disclosure of confidential information.

(2) The insertion of a restraint of trade clause
The second exception to an ex-employee's freedom to go into competition with his/her former employer may be the insertion of a restraint of trade clause in the contract of employment.

Only such interests as trade secrets, the stability of the workforce and customer connections may be protected by such a clause.

The restrictive covenant must be shown to go no further – in terms of scope, time and area of the restraint – than is reasonable, and it must generally be in the public interest: see *Littlewoods Organisation Ltd v Harris* [1978]; *Greer v Sketchley Ltd* [1979]. In *Kynixa Ltd v Hines* [2008] the High Court held that a restrictive covenant for a period of 12 months following employment, and which was very wide in scope, was reasonable and enforceable. This in part was due to the senior positions that the three employees held and that they had been in breach of their fiduciary duties.

The courts will not generally re-write clauses which offend against the above, and any clauses which are ambiguous may be subject to the *contra proferentem* rule – it will be interpreted strictly against the party seeking to rely upon it (*Home Counties Dairies v Skilton* [1970]). Wrongful dismissal invalidates an otherwise enforceable covenant: *Rock Refrigeration Ltd v Jones* [1996].

Restraint of trade clauses are subject to the doctrine of severance (more commonly referred to as the 'blue pencil' test) and 'blue pencilling' is used where a restraining clause is too broad or aspects of it are unlawful. The tests for severance were defined in *Sadler v Imperial Life Assurance of Canada* [1988] as requiring: 1) The ability to remove the words without requiring the addition or alteration of the remaining aspects of the clause; 2) the remaining clause continues to make grammatical sense; and 3) the removal of the words does not alter the nature of the original clause.

'GARDEN LEAVE'
See, particularly:

- *Evening Standard Ltd v Henderson* [1987];

- *Rex Stewart Ltd v Parker* [1988];

- *Provincial Financial Group plc v Hayward* [1989].

A garden leave clause will not be necessary where the employer has a contractual right to prevent the employee from coming into work and the employer is not under a duty to provide work: *William Hill Organisation Ltd v Tucker* [1999].

The High Court held in *SG&R Valuation Service v Boudrais* [2008] that a garden leave term may be implied into contracts of senior directors where no such right exists in the contract (and granted an injunction to this effect). An employee's implied right to work (see below) is subject to the qualification that he/she has not, by some prior breach of contract or wider duty, rendered it impossible/ reasonably impracticable for the employer to provide work. Here the directors had done just that and therefore they had no right to be provided with work by the former employer.

The Court of Appeal, in *Garratt v Mirror Group Newspapers Ltd* [2011] provided interesting guidance on when a term may be implied into an employment contract regarding the requirement to sign a compromise agreement before the employee could receive an enhanced redundancy payment.

Not to impede the employer's business
See *Secretary of State for Employment v ASLEF (No 2)* [1972] and *British Telecommunications plc v Ticehurst* [1992].

> ### ▶ SECRETARY OF STATE FOR EMPLOYMENT v ASLEF (NO 2) [1972]
>
> The case involved an instruction from the ASLEF trade union to its members to take part in industrial action by performing a 'work to rule'.
>
> This resulted in the exact instructions for employees in the works' handbook being followed and included refusing overtime and rest-day working. The action was aimed at disrupting the employer's work rather than protecting the employees' health and safety.
>
> It was held by the Court of Appeal that even by following the contract, the employees had breached their implied obligation to serve their employer faithfully.

To cooperate with the employer
Employees have the duty of cooperation and must work with their employer in the best interests of the business. This goes beyond adherence to a textual reading of the contract of employment, and if the employee's action is used to cause harm to the employer, the employee will breach the duty. See *Secretary of State for Employment v ASLEF (No 2)* [1972].

Maintain mutual trust and confidence

The employee may not breach the duty to maintain the respect between themselves and the employer. See *Donovan v Invicta Airways Ltd* [1970]; and *Mahmud v Bank of Credit and Commerce International SA* [1998].

HOW TERMS ARE IMPLIED INTO THE CONTRACT

Terms may be implied through the courts, custom and practice and through Parliament's intervention.

Courts

The two main reasons for the courts implying terms has been, first, due to business efficacy; and secondly, because the term was so obvious each party must have assumed it would be included.

The courts implied a term to give business efficacy to the contract as demonstrated in *The Moorcock* [1889].

The second type of term that a court may be willing to imply is where the term is so obvious that the parties clearly intended it to be included. See *Shirlaw v Southern Foundries Ltd* [1939].

Custom and practice

For custom to have a legal effect, it must be reasonable, certain and notorious. Does the worker have to be aware of the custom? See *Sagar v Ridehalgh & Son* [1931]; cf *Meek v Port of London Authority* [1918]; *Quinn v Calder Industrial Materials Ltd* [1996].

Statute

See statutory implied terms giving rights: guaranteed pay, equal pay and minimum notice. Also, see the law on working time, which, in general, imposes a ceiling of 48 hours on working time per week. There are exceptions.

The National Minimum Wage Act 1998 overrides arrangements to pay less than the minimum. Also, on occasion, statute will render a contractual term void (s 203 of the ERA 1996).

Note that there are special rules governing the payment of wages (Pt II of the ERA 1996).

THE WORKING TIME REGULATIONS 1998

The Working Time Regulations (WTR) 1998 provide protection for workers, following the Working Time Directive 1993, by providing a maximum working week and minimum rest and break periods. However, the Regulations are subject to an opt-out scheme (regs 4 and 5) whereby workers can choose, in writing, not to enforce their rights. This is subject to a requirement that workers are allowed to opt-in if they subsequently change their mind.

Working time

For the purposes of the WTR 1998, working time is calculated as any period during which the worker is working, at the employers disposal and carrying out the worker's activities/duties. Any time during which the worker is receiving relevant training; and any additional period which is to be treated as working time for the purposes of the Regulations (reg 2 of WTR 1998).

The maximum working time for the purposes of the Regulations is 48 hours per week, calculated as an average over a 17-week period (reg 4).

Rest breaks

The Regulations provide that an adult worker is entitled to a 20-minute rest break if expected to work more than six hours at a stretch. Further, he/she is entitled to 11 hours' rest in each 24-hour period, and 12 hours' rest is applicable for young workers (reg 10).

Annual leave

The Regulations provided for the introduction of a system of paid annual leave that has resulted in entitlement to 5.6 weeks from 1st April 2009 to reflect 20 days of holidays and 8 days of statutory bank holidays (reg 13). Note that such leave may be lost at the end of a year where it has not been taken (*Lyons v Mitie Security Ltd* [2010]).

The employer is obliged to clearly distinguish between 'normal' pay, and pay for leave as provided in lieu of holidays. Previously, it had been a common practice of employers to 'roll up' pay with pay in lieu and hence circumvent the requirement to allow workers to take their holidays. The Court of Justice provided this clear identification of how the pay received by the worker was to be declared separately as pay for work, and pay for holiday entitlement (*Robinson-Steele v RD Retail Services Ltd* [2006]).

An employer cannot consider sick leave to be part of a worker's annual leave (the Court of Justice in *Pereda v Madrid Movilidad SA* [2009]).

Night workers

The Regulations are also applicable to workers employed on shift patterns and night work. This assessment is concerned with the regularity of the period of night work rather than whether it involves the majority of the work. Reg 6 provides that night workers should not exceed eight hours work in any 24-hour period (albeit that this is assessed over an average of 17 weeks).

Enforcement

An employer who refuses to allow a worker to gain access to protection, or does not take reasonable steps to ensure compliance with the WTR 1998, is guilty of a criminal offence. This is extended to an employer who dismisses or treats less favourably, a worker for exercising, or attempting to exercise, his/her rights.

Employers are only required to hold general records regarding workers' hours of work and written documentation. However, the Court of Justice provided a strong recommendation that it may be in the employers' interest to hold sufficient records to demonstrate that any opt-out was expressed (see *Pfeiffer v Deutsches Rotes Kreuz Kreisverband Waldshut eV* [2004]), rather than implied, and was, along with any other contractual term, entered into freely (*Barber v RJB Mining* [1999]).

You should now be confident that you would be able to tick all the boxes on the checklist at the beginning of this chapter. To check your knowledge of The contract of employment why not visit the companion website and take the Multiple Choice Question test. Check your understanding of the terms and vocabulary used in this chapter with the flashcard glossary.

2

Equal pay

All contracts of employment are deemed to include
an equality clause

English law (the Equality Act 2010) is to be interpreted in
conformity with European Community laws (Article 141
and the Equal Pay Directive)

The term 'pay' includes any consideration that the worker
receives from the employer (such as sick leave, pension
contributions, holiday pay etc)

There are the three 'heads' under which a claim can be
made – like work; work rated as equivalent; and work of
equal value

Claims have to be made using a comparator from the 'same
employment'

The comparator may be a predecessor (and possibly (again)
a successor following the Equality Act 2010) but he/she must
be a member of the opposite sex

Equal value claims can include a claimant who has been rated
as performing 'higher' work (not equal work) than the comparator

The employer can raise a 'material factor' defence that a
difference in pay is not due to sex of the claimant

A claim must be made (in most circumstances) within six months
of leaving employment (or any time during)

The award following a successful claim may be
back-dated up to six years

There is no qualification period to claim under the law

THE MAIN SOURCES OF LAW

The main sources of law relating to equality between men and women in terms of pay are now contained in the Equality Act (EA) 2010. The EA 2010 repealed much of the previous laws – Equal Pay Act (EPA) 1970; Equal Pay Act 1970 (Amendment) Regulations 2003; and the Race Relations Act 1976 which dealt with inequality in pay based on race: *Wakeman v Quick Corp* [1999].

The European Union laws applicable to equal pay still apply and are contained in:

- Article 141 of the European Community (EC) Treaty;
- Directive 75/117 (the Equal Pay Directive).

EUROPEAN COMMUNITY LAW

The European Community (EC) continues to have a significant effect on equality and discrimination laws and English law must always be considered along with EC law and judgments from the Court of Justice (of the European Union).

Article 141 of the Treaty establishes the principle of equal pay for equal work. The Article is directly applicable (enforceable) in the Member States and takes precedence over domestic law. It has to be interpreted subject to the Equal Pay Directive, which fleshes it out. Whilst the Directive is not directly enforceable against individual employers (as there is no 'horizontal' direct effect of directives), Art 141 must be interpreted in accordance with it; consequently it is, in effect, applied directly.

THE MEANING OF 'PAY'

'Pay' is defined under Art 141 as any 'consideration whether in cash or in kind, which the worker receives directly or indirectly, in respect of his employment, from his employer.'

It includes wages and other terms and conditions in employment such as bonus payments, holiday provisions, sick leave, employer's pension contributions and redundancy payments.

'Equal pay' means for the 'same work or for work to which equal value is attributed' (Art 141).

Article 141 is directly enforceable in the national courts: *Jenkins v Kingsgate (Clothing Productions) Ltd* [1981]. It was held by the Court of Appeal in *Barber v Staffordshire County Council* [1996], that the effect of Art 141 is to modify any provisions that conflict with domestic legislation.

The EA 2010 must be interpreted in the light of Art 141 to ensure consistency of approach: *Pickstone v Freemans plc* [1989]. If, however, domestic law provides an adequate remedy, then EC law will not be directly enforceable by the complainant: *Blaik v Post Office* [1994].

The meaning of the word 'pay' in EC law has been interpreted in a flexible way, providing additional scope to the domestic legislative provisions. For example, 'pay' may include:

- benefits paid under a contracted out occupational pension scheme (*Barber v Guardian Royal Exchange Assurance Group* [1991]);

- sick pay (*Rinner-Kühn v FWW Spezial-Gebäudereinigung GmbH* [1989]);

- concessionary rail travel (*Garland v British Rail Engineering Ltd* [1982]);

- piecework schemes (*Specialarbejderforbundet i Danmark v Dansk Industrie (acting for Copenhagen A/S)* [1995]);

- compensation for unfair dismissal (*R v Secretary of State for Employment ex p Seymour-Smith* [1999]).

▶ R v SECRETARY OF STATE FOR EMPLOYMENT ex p SEYMOUR-SMITH [1999]

The case involved a woman who wished to lodge an unfair dismissal claim, but was not permitted as she required two years' continuous service under the Unfair Dismissal (Variation of Qualifying Period) Order 1985.

Seymour-Smith claimed this law was contrary to the EC's principle of equal treatment as it was more difficult for women to accrue the two years' continuous service than men, and hence indirectly discriminated against them.

The House of Lords referred the matter to the Court of Justice which held that the judicial payment of compensation under the domestic law was pay under the definition of Art 119 (now Art 141 EC). The legislation, as a consequence, was changed and the qualification period reduced to one year's continuous service.

EQUALITY ACT 2010

WHO DOES THE ACT COVER?

The Act applies to **men and women** who are employed in Great Britain (s 11(a)).

'Employed' is defined in s 83(2) as a person employed under a contract of service or apprenticeship, or those under a contract personally to do any work. Therefore, its scope is broad and it is not restricted to those with 'employee' status.

The claimant can be employed full-time and part-time, there is no qualification period to gain access to the right, and it covers those working in large and small organisations.

It applies to workers of all ages.

The EA 2010 s 66(1) implies an equality clause into every contract of employment and the parties cannot waive the right.

The equality clause will operate to equalise pay related terms in a contract of employment where there is a man and woman employed on:

- like work;
- work rated equivalent;
- work of equal value.

THE MEANING OF 'PAY' WITHIN THE EA 2010

Each term of the remuneration package should be considered individually and should be equalised (*Hayward v Cammell Laird Shipbuilders* [1988]), even though this may give rise to 'leapfrogging/piggyback claims' (mutual enhancement). This approach, whilst controversial, is allowed as confirmed by the Employment Appeal Tribunal (EAT) in *South Tyneside Borough Council v McAvoy*

Et Ors [2009]. As a consequence, even though the same pay is being provided to men and women, benefits such as health insurance, a company car and so on, are included in the assessment.

> ### ▶ HAYWARD v CAMMELL LAIRD SHIPBUILDERS [1988]
>
> The case involved a woman employed as a cook who brought a claim based on equal value with three male comparators employed as a painter, joiner and engineer respectively.
>
> It was agreed between the parties that Hayward received less favourable treatment than the men, but when her contract was viewed as a whole (including sickness benefits and meal breaks) she was treated as favourably.
>
> The House of Lords held that the EPA 1970, s 1(2) (now EA 2010 s 65) provided that each term of the contract was to be viewed and made not less favourable for the woman, irrespective of whether the whole contract provided her to be treated as favourably.

Occupational benefits fall within the meaning of the word 'pay' (*Griffin v London Pension Fund Authority* [1993]); redundancy and *ex gratia* payments are also included (*McKechnie v UBM Building Supplies (Southern) Ltd* [1991]).

THE COMPARATOR

▧ Any claim must be brought by a member of the opposite sex.

▧ The EPA 1970 required claimants to use an actual comparator rather than a hypothetical one. The EA 2010 also allows for the use of a hypothetical comparator where no actual comparator exists and where the claim relates to direct discrimination.

▧ The comparator is someone who is employed in the same employment as the comparator, that is, either by the same employer or an associated employer, and either at the same establishment or at an establishment where common terms and conditions are observed (such as an employer's parent company) (s 79 of the EA 2010). In *Beddoes & Ors v Birmingham City Council* [2010] the EAT held that the words 'same employment' should be construed naturally. Further, in *City of Edinburgh v Wilkinson & Ors* [2010] the EAT held that a broad approach of 'same employment' was to be taken when interpreting its application to the claimant and the comparator. This should not be restricted to an assessment of whether the work was undertaken in only one geographic location.

■ Predecessors may be comparators (*Macarthys Ltd v Smith* [1981]). Whilst case law under the EPA 1970 provided that successors could not be used as comparators, it appears that the EA 2010 does allow for such comparators to be used. This will be tested in the coming months and years.

■ 'Employed' means employed either under a contract of service or a contract personally to execute work. If this is the major obligation under the contract, then the contract falls within the EA 2010 (*Mirror Group Newspapers Ltd v Gunning* [1986]).

■ 'Common terms and conditions' means terms and conditions which are substantially comparable on a broad basis. It is, therefore, sufficient for the applicant to show that his/her comparators at another establishment or at his/her establishment were employed on broadly similar terms (*British Coal Corp v Smith* [1996]).

■ Article 141 extends the range of comparators to those employed in the same establishment or service (*Scullard v Knowles* [1996]), but cannot be used to compare completely different organisations (*Lawrence v Regent Office Care Ltd* [1999]; *Allonby v Accrington & Rossendale College* [2001]); however, be aware of *South Ayrshire Council v Morton* [2002]; *Robertson v DEFRA* [2005].

■ Women are no longer required to name a specific male employee as a comparator when filing an equal pay grievance (*Hurst v Suffolk Mental Health Trust and Arnold* [2009] and *Others v Sandwell Metropolitan Borough Council* [2009]);

■ Multi-comparators are allowed (*Langley v Beecham Proprietories* [1985]).

> ▶ MACARTHYS LTD v SMITH [1981]
>
> The case involved Mrs Smith who wished to bring an equal pay claim against her male predecessor who had been paid a higher salary for work of equal value.
>
> In fulfilling the obligations on Member States under EC law, the Court of Appeal had to construe and apply the EPA 1970 in a way that was compatible with Art 119 (now Art 141 EC).

- Comparison with a successor had previously been permitted (*Diocese of Hallam Trustees v Connaughton* [1996]). EPA 1970 did not include a provision for a comparator to be someone appointed after the claimant, the tribunal decided that it had jurisdiction to hear the claim based on Art 119 of the EC Treaty (now Art 141) and the Employment Appeal Tribunal (EAT) confirmed this jurisdiction;

- An order for discovery may be obtained in order to identify the most appropriate comparator (*Leverton v Clwyd CC* [1989]); however, this may not be used as the right to undertake a 'fishing trip' to identify possible claims.

THE HEADS OF CLAIM

LIKE WORK

The applicant must show that he/she is employed on 'like work' with the comparator (s 65(1)(a) of EA 2010). The work should, therefore, be the same or of a broadly similar nature. Differences which are not of practical importance can actually be disregarded. This allows the adoption of a 'broad brush' approach. For example, in *Electrolux Ltd v Hutchinson* [1977], male employees were paid a higher piecework rate for doing work of a broadly similar nature to female employees. However, the men could be asked to do more demanding work, to work nights and to do non-production work. The issue was whether these extra duties justified a higher rate of pay. The EAT concluded that they did not. The frequency with which they were asked to undertake this extra work was relevant, and this would have to be very frequent if the difference in pay was to be justified.

The following may be relevant:

■ additional responsibility may justify a difference in pay (*Eaton Ltd v Nuttall* [1977]);

■ the tribunal must consider what actually happens in practice, rather than what is contained in the job description (*Shields v E Coomes (Holdings) Ltd* [1978]);

■ the time at which work is carried out is not normally relevant, unless it brings with it additional responsibilities (*Dugdale v Kraft Foods Ltd* [1977]; *Thomas v National Coal Board* [1987]);

■ where an applicant is employed on work of a higher value than that of the comparator, terms should be equalised, but he/she is not entitled to a higher wage (*Murphy v An Bord Telecom Eireann* [1988]).

WORK RATED EQUIVALENT

Employers cannot be compelled to undertake a job evaluation study, but where such a study has taken place, the claimant can use the findings in his/her claim (s 65(4) of EA 2010).

Job evaluations must satisfy the requirements of:

■ having been analytical;

■ having been objectively assessed to identify the value placed on the work performed (skill, responsibility and so on);

■ having analysed the claimant's job and the job of a comparator; and

■ having been conducted at the undertaking where the claimant is employed.

This head of claim is dependent upon the employer having carried out a job evaluation scheme. If the scheme is an analytical scheme, in which the woman's work and the man's work have been rated as equivalent, then pay and other contractual terms must be the same (s 66(2) of EA 2010). If the conclusion is to the contrary, then an applicant will not succeed in his or her claim for either 'like work' or 'work of equal value'. However, if the job evaluation scheme was not analytical or was discriminatory, an equal value claim may succeed. An analytical scheme should consider all matters connected with the nature of the work, including effort, skills and responsibilities: *Eaton Ltd v Nuttall* [1977].

> ▶ EATON LTD v NUTTALL [1977]
>
> Here the EAT considered a situation where an employer had performed a job evaluation study and as a consequence based salary grades on the findings to a minimum, mid and maximum point scale. Where the workers were placed on the scale depended on the management's assessment of factors such as the worker's responsibility.
>
> As this involved a subjective decision by the management, the EAT held that the study had failed under s 1(5) of EPA 1970, as a valid study requires the worker to be able to apply the consequences of the study to arrive at their point on the salary scale developed.

Analytical schemes include: *points assessment*, which breaks down each job into a number of factors, points being awarded for each factor on a pre-determined scale; and *factor comparison*, in which the evaluation is based on a limited number of factors, such as skills and responsibilities.

Non-analytical schemes include: *job ranking*, in which a ranking table of jobs is produced and the ranked jobs are grouped into grades; and *paired comparison*, in which one job is compared to another and, thereby, awarded points.

Where the claim is for 'work rated as equivalent' this involves both 'equivalent' work and work which has rated the claimant as performing 'higher' work than the comparator: *Bainbridge (No 1) v Redcar & Cleveland Borough Council* [2007].

> ▶ BAINBRIDGE (No 1) v REDCAR & CLEVELAND BOROUGH COUNCIL [2007]
>
> This case involved women workers who compared themselves with men and had been rated as performing equivalent, and in some instances 'higher', work. However, the women were paid less due to bonuses and 'attendance allowances' given to the men that created a disparate impact – a point conceded by the employer. A defence raised was that the legislation required a claim for 'work rated as equivalent' rather than work which had been rated as being higher.

The Court of Appeal held that the relevant section of the EPA 1970 should be changed to enable a claim to be made where a job evaluation study has found the worker to be performing equivalent, and higher, rated work with his/her comparator.

In addition, schemes may contain discriminatory job factors, such as dexterity or strength, which would allow the job evaluation scheme to be challenged under both the EA 2010 and the Equal Pay Directive (*Rummler v Dato-Druck GmbH* [1987]).

If a company has a clear and non-discriminatory job evaluation scheme in place, this does of course provide the basis for a good defence to any claim for equal pay.

WORK OF EQUAL VALUE

The work of equal value provision allows the applicant to claim the same pay as the comparator if he/she is doing work of the same value in terms of the demands made on him/her (s 65(6)(b) of EA 2010). Equal value includes factors such as the demands of the job; responsibility; decision-making; effort; and skill.

Following the decision in *Pickstone v Freemans plc* [1989], an equal value claim may be made even though there is (for example) a man employed in the same job as the woman. This prevents an employer from using the 'token man' to block an equal value claim. However, where there is a genuine 'like work' claim, it is usually in the applicant's interest to pursue this course of action, as, in terms of procedure, such claims are less complicated than equal value claims.

PROCEDURE FOR CLAIMS OF EQUAL VALUE

What amounts to equal value?

The issue for the tribunal is whether to adopt a narrow or broad-brush approach. For example, if the independent expert has reported that the applicant's job is valued at 97 per cent of the comparator's job, is this work of equal value? If a broad-brush approach is taken, it probably is. The current trend appears to be to adopt the broad-brush approach: *Pickstone v Freemans plc* [1989].

Procedure for claims of equal value

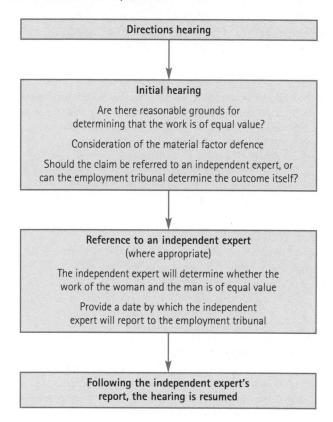

Directions hearing

Initial hearing

Are there reasonable grounds for
determining that the work is of equal value?

Consideration of the material factor defence

Should the claim be referred to an independent expert, or
can the employment tribunal determine the outcome itself?

Reference to an independent expert
(where appropriate)

The independent expert will determine whether the
work of the woman and the man is of equal value

Provide a date by which the independent
expert will report to the employment tribunal

**Following the independent expert's
report, the hearing is resumed**

MATERIAL FACTOR DEFENCE

The burden of proof is on the applicant to establish that his/her work falls
within either the like work, work rated as equivalent, or work of equal value
provisions. Even where the applicant succeeds in this, the employer may still be
able to avoid equalising terms by establishing the material factor defence.

The EPA 1970 used the words 'genuine material factor' which have been
replaced with a 'material factor' defence in s 69 of EA 2010. There should not be

any real change with the removal of the word 'genuine'. Indeed it has been suggested the word was removed to avoid the confusion often provoked by its existence. The employer will continue to have to demonstrate the factor is genuine and not a sham, and a factor is not material unless it is a material difference between the claimant and comparator's case (s 69(6) of EA 2010).

This defence allows the employer to prove that the variation in pay is genuinely due to a material factor other than sex. If the difference is not based on sex, no justification need be provided: *Strathclyde Regional Council v Wallace* [1998].

> ▶ **STRATHCLYDE REGIONAL COUNCIL v WALLACE [1998]**
>
> The case involved Wallace and other women workers employed by the Council as teachers who performed the same role as principal teachers, but who received wages at a lower rate.
>
> In the tribunal, the Council had relied on the defence under s 1(3) of EPA 1970, and it was held by the House of Lords that this was legitimate insofar as the genuine factors relied on for the difference in pay was not due to the sex of the workers. It is only in circumstances where the factor could be directly or indirectly discriminatory that the employer would have to objectively justify the pay disparity.

An important development of s 69 of EA 2010 appears to be necessity of the employer demonstrating an objective justification for the difference in pay (s 69(3) of EA 2010). This will be required in all cases, even where there is no element of sex discrimination. As such, the approach adopted in *Wallace* is subsequently of questionable authority. .

What amounts to a 'material factor/difference'?
The difference in pay must be objectively justified. This requires the employer to demonstrate that the difference corresponds directly to a 'real' need and to achieve a business objective, and is proportionate to that end.

RED-CIRCLE AGREEMENTS

These allow the employer to protect the salary of an employee or group of employees, even though they may have been moved to a lower grade of work (usually after the completion of a job evaluation study): *Snoxell v Vauxhall Motors Ltd* [1977].

> ### ▶ SNOXELL v VAUXHALL MOTORS LTD [1977]
>
> The case involved men and women workers at Vauxhall employed as quality controllers. Whilst performing like work, the women were placed in a lower grade and paid at a lower rate than the men.
>
> As the organisation was preparing for the full implementation of the EPA 1970 it began a process of re-assessing roles and the role of quality controller was downgraded. However, the women workers were placed on the new 'lower' rate, whilst the men were 'red circled' and hence kept at their higher rate.
>
> The EAT held that this amounted to discrimination in the red circling procedure as the women were performing 'like work' with the men, and hence this could not be used as a defence.

DIFFERENT GEOGRAPHICAL AREAS

Different rates of pay or salaries may be justifiable for different locations: see *NAAFI v Varley* [1977].

SENIORITY: EXPERIENCE

This may justify a difference in pay, even though it might also discriminate against women whose careers may be interrupted due to care responsibilities: see *Nimz v Freie und Hansestadt Hamburg* [1991]. This position was confirmed as a matter of EC law by the Court of Justice in *Cadman v Health and Safety Executive* [2006].

SKILL AND QUALIFICATIONS

See *Clay Cross (Quarry Services) Ltd v Fletcher* [1979].

ADDITIONAL RESPONSIBILITY

Where the difference in pay is based on additional responsibilities, there must be actual and frequent tasks: *Shields v E Coomes (Holdings) Ltd* [1978].

▶ SHIELDS v E COOMES (HOLDINGS) LTD [1978]

The case involved a female employee who worked in a betting shop. She was paid less than the male employees performing the same job on the basis, the employers contended, that the men acted as security guards at the organisation. If there was any trouble, the men acted as deterrents, even though in reality there had never been a situation which called on the men to act in this capacity.

The Court of Appeal held that the practical differences between the jobs of the woman and the men were negligible, and hence the difference in pay was due to the sex of the employees.

MARKET FORCES

This may be an acceptable defence where there are genuine economic factors which affect, or have an impact upon, the employer's business: *Rainey v Greater Glasgow Health Board* [1987]. However, the need to undertake compulsory competitive tendering is not an automatic defence: *Ratcliffe v North Yorkshire CC* [1995]. Obviously, unlimited use of a market forces defence would totally undermine the effectiveness of the EA 2010 – there will always, therefore, be a conflict between the purpose of the statute and market forces.

▶ RAINEY v GREATER GLASGOW HEALTH BOARD [1987]

Here the Board was required to establish a prosthesis service in place of existing arrangements with contractors in the private sector.

As such, the Board considered that the current pay scales may be insufficient to attract suitably qualified prosthetists. Therefore a system was established whereby those employees coming from the private sector would have their previous salary matched, but remuneration in general was to be related to standard pay scales. Rainey was paid according to the standard scales while a similarly qualified male employee joining from the private sector was paid much higher wages.

The House of Lords held that the difference in pay was not due to the sex of the workers, but rather due to a 'sound administrative reason' and hence justifiable.

COLLECTIVE BARGAINING AND SEPARATE PAY STRUCTURES

These are not necessarily an automatic defence: *British Coal Corp v Smith* [1996]; *Enderby v Frenchay Health Authority* [1994].

Following the decision in *Handels-og Kontorfunktionaerernes Forbund i Danmark v Dansk Arbejdsgiverforening (Acting for Danfoss)* [1989], it is clear that pay systems should be transparent so that it is clear to all parties why they are on a particular grade. In the absence of transparency, the burden of proof is on the employer to show that there is no discrimination. The mere existence of separate pay structures based on different collective agreements does not necessarily amount to an objective justification: *British Road Services v Loughran* [1997].

An example of an employer failing in its defence is *North Yorkshire County Council v Ratcliffe* [1995], where the House of Lords ruled that a variation in pay occasioned by compulsory competitive tendering was not justified.

TIME LIMITS AND COMPENSATION

Limits imposed on claims for equal pay are as follows:

- Compensation in equal pay claims was previously limited to up to two years' back pay (s 2(5) of the EPA 1970). However, this provision was challenged in the case of *Levez v PH Jennings (Harlow Pools) Ltd* [1999]. Here the Court of Justice held that due to the deceit of the employer (which misled the employee), the two-year rule would have made it excessively difficult for the employee to enforce her rights.

▨ Consequently, under the Equal Pay Act (Amendment) Regulations 2003, the limit on back-dated equal pay claims was raised to six years to fall in line with claims under breach of contract.

▨ A claim for equal pay can be made at any time while the worker is employed.

▨ If the worker has left employment, the time limit for bringing claims is six months. A ruling by the Court of Justice in *Preston v Wolverhampton Health Care NHS Trust* [2001] provided that the six-month rule is appropriate, but this period may be extended in two circumstances: where an employer has deliberately concealed from the claimant any fact relevant to his/her claim (and the claimant did not or could not have reasonably discovered this during employment); or the claimant was under a disability during the six months following, having left employment when the claim would otherwise have been presented.

▨ In the event of any fact being concealed from the claimant, the six-month period does not begin until the claimant discovered, or reasonably should have discovered, the fact.

▨ In the event of a disability preventing the presentation of a claim, the six-month period does not begin until the claimant has ceased to be under the disability.

▨ Following the Court of Justice's decision in *Preston* [2001], a claimant employed under a 'stable employment relationship' can claim throughout the employment, or may use the six-month rule to claim at the end of the entire employment, rather than bring separate claims at the conclusion of each individual contract of employment.

 ● In *Ashby & Ors v Birmingham City Council* [2011] the High Court determined that (under the old EPA 1970 s 2(3)) claimants were not prevented from having equal pay claims heard in the civil courts where they were out of time for the case to be heard in the employment tribunals. If it was reasonable for the claim not to be presented in the tribunal, it may be that the interests of justice would be served by the case being heard in the civil courts.

PRIOR TO THE COMPLAINT

GATHERING INFORMATION

It is not a legal necessity, but may be prudent to use the equal pay questionnaire to determine whether a worker has a claim for equal pay.

The questionnaire will help the claimant to establish the facts that will determine, in the first instance, whether a claim should/can be pursued.

The employer must respond to the questionnaire within eight weeks of being presented with it. Failure to provide the information without a justifiable reason (such as confidential information) will be viewed negatively by the tribunal.

To use the information in a tribunal claim, the questionnaire must be served to the employer before the complaint is presented to the tribunal or within 21 days after making a claim to the tribunal.

You should now be confident that you would be able to tick all the boxes on the checklist at the beginning of this chapter. To check your knowledge of Equal pay why not visit the companion website and take the Multiple Choice Question test. Check your understanding of the terms and vocabulary used in this chapter with the flashcard glossary.

Discrimination

Sex discrimination legislation has effect before, during and after employment	
English law must be interpreted in conformity with European Community law	
Protection against prohibited conduct applies to individuals with a protected characteristic	
Discrimination may be direct; indirect; harassment or victimisation	
Direct discrimination involves treating a worker less favourably due to his/her protected characteristic	
Direct discrimination (in most instances) cannot be justified and the motives of the employer are irrelevant	
A comparator is required to establish a claim	
Claims have to be made within three months of the last complained of act of discrimination	
Indirect discrimination can be justified if there are objective and reasonable grounds	
Employers may be held vicariously liable for actions that amount to discrimination	

THE MAIN SOURCES OF LAW

The main sources of law relating to discrimination were significantly changed following commencement of the Equality Act (EA) 2010. The former laws (with the exception of the EC laws) as identified below were repealed either in part or their entirety:

- Sex Discrimination Act (SDA) 1975 (repealed in its entirety);

- Employment Equality (Sexual Orientation) Regulations 2003 (repealed in its entirety);

- EC Directive 76/207 (the Equal Treatment Directive), that covers sex discrimination only;

- EC Equal Treatment Framework Directive (2000/78);

- Employment Equality (Religion or Belief) Regulations 2003 (SI 2003/1660) (repealed in its entirety);

- Race Relations Act (RRA) 1976 (repealed in its entirety);

- Disability Discrimination Act (DDA) 1995 (repealed in part);

- Employment Equality (Age) Regulations 2006 (repealed in its entirety).

EUROPEAN COMMUNITY LAW

EC law has had a significant impact in the field of discrimination, through the various directives and the decisions of the Court of Justice (of the European Union). Directives may be enforced directly in the UK national courts against the State or an organ of the State as an employer, but not against a private employer (there is no horizontal direct effect of Directives). *Foster v British Gas plc* [1991] established that an 'organ or emanation of the State' was held to include a body which has been made responsible for providing a public service under the control of the State and has, for that purpose, special powers beyond those which result from the normal rules applicable in relations between private individuals. One significant change resulting from the application of Directive 76/207 was the equalisation of retirement ages for men and women: *Marshall v Southampton and South West Hampshire AHA (Teaching)* [1986].

Although EC law has provided flexibility and additional scope in interpreting English law (through its purposive approach to statutory interpretation), it does not extend to positive discrimination. In *Kalanke v Freie und Hansestadt Bremen* [1995], an automatic preference for the hiring of a female candidate was held to be unlawful. However, a preference for a female in a job where women are underrepresented is lawful if the individual circumstances of the male applicant can be taken into account (positive action): *Marschall v Land Nordrhein Westfalen* [1998]. By virtue of the Treaty of Amsterdam 1997, the EC has competence in the field of race discrimination.

Employment tribunals have the jurisdiction to hear and determine disputes arising directly from EC legislation (*Impact v Minister for Agriculture and Food (Ireland)* [2008]).

ENGLISH LAW

The EA 2010 came into force on 1st October 2010 which codified existing equality laws and the decisions of the Court of Justice (of the European Union). This major piece of legislation has had significant effects on the provision of the law. Previous laws were spread over many pieces of legislation and statutory instruments, interpreted by domestic and EU case law. Hence the EA 2010 harmonises the law – using new terms and definitions that are widely applicable to all forms of discrimination. This is intended to simply the provision of equality law.

Discrimination is unlawful if it is based on one of the protected characteristics as established in the EA 2010:

- race (s 9);
- sex (s 11);
- sexual orientation (s 12);
- marriage and civil partnership (s 8);
- disability (s 6);
- religion or belief (s 10);
    - age (s 5);
    - gender reassignment (s 7)
    - pregnancy and maternity (ss 72–76)

PROTECTED CHARACTERISTICS

SEX AND RACE

The EA 2010 provides protection against discrimination based on sex or race to workers (see Chapter 2) – those who carry out the employment personally.

There is no qualification period necessary to qualify and awards of damages are not subject to a maximum or cap.

The protected characteristic of sex is defined in s 11 of EA 2010 – a reference to a person who has this particular protected characteristic is a reference to a man or to a woman; or to persons of the same sex.

There are no changes to the protection already provided in relation to a person's race. Race is defined in s 9 of EA 2010 as including colour; nationality; and ethnic or national origins.

■ The protected characteristic refers to a person of a particular racial group or persons of the same racial group.

■ Simply because a racial group comprises two or more distinct racial groups does not prevent it from constituting a particular racial group (s 8(4)).

■ A power granted to a Minister of the Crown is to amend this section to provide (or not) for caste to be an aspect of race (s 8(5)).

Each of the forms of prohibited conduct are applicable to discrimination based on a person's sex or race. It is also unlawful for an employer to instruct another person to discriminate on his/her behalf.

Comparator

The claimant must demonstrate he/she has been victim of less favourable treatment due to his/her sex or race than a person without the protected characteristic. Hypothetical comparators may be used and the question to be asked is 'but for the relevant protected characteristic, would the claimant have been treated in that way?'

A comparator is not needed in cases of racial segregation (s 13(1) EA 2010).

THE RACIAL AND RELIGIOUS HATRED ACT 2006

This Act came into force on 1st October 2007 and seeks to broaden the scope of protection from the crime of incitement to commit racial hatred by extending this also to religious hatred.

The Act creates an offence in the use of words and behaviour that amounts to a threat and that intends to stir up religious hatred against a group of people that are defined by their religious belief or lack of belief. The Act now helps to protect groups such as Muslims, Rastafarians, Christians and other groups who were not included in the definition provided in the legislation prohibiting incitement of racial hatred that protected groups such as Jews and Sikhs.

Importantly, the Act establishes that individuals and corporations can be guilty, and in the case of a corporation if 'it is shown that the offence was committed with the consent or connivance of a director, manager, secretary or other similar officer' (Public Order Act 1985, s 29M(1)).

Punishment under the Act includes a fine or imprisonment of up to seven years.

SEX AND SEXUAL ORIENTATION

The EA 2010 has replaced the Employment Equality (Sexual Orientation) Regulations 2003 which protect against discrimination on the basis of a person's sexual orientation (s 12). It covers individuals whose orientation is towards persons of the same sex, opposite sex, or both sexes.

The EA 2010 prohibits unwanted conduct on the basis of the person's actual or perceived sexual orientation, and less favourable treatment. In *Lisboa v Realpubs Ltd* [2011], the EAT held that less favourable treatment is sufficiently wide to cover any situation where a person's sexual orientation is an effective cause of the detriment suffered.

The EA 2010 provides a genuine occupational requirement defence where a particular sexual orientation is a genuine and determining occupational requirement and the discrimination is proportionate to achieve this aim. This is most commonly seen in the case of employment at organised religions.

MARRIAGE OR CIVIL PARTNERSHIP STATUS

The EA 2010 prohibits discrimination on the basis of an individual's marital/ co-habitation status. In direct discrimination in employment related to marriage/ civil partnership, the direct discrimination only covers less favourable treatment because the worker is married or has a civil partner. Single people or those in relationships outside of these protected characteristics are not covered.

DISABILITY

Employers had been under specific duties to protect against discrimination on the basis of a person's disability. This not only applied to employers, but to a wider group of service providers.

A key aspect of reducing discrimination faced by individuals is for (in the respect of this book) employers to make reasonable adjustments to their business so person's with disabilities may have access to buildings, services and so on.

Since 2004, all employers have been required to produce a Disability Equality Policy regarding elements such as employment policies, training and education facilities, information, services, consultations with representatives and so on.

The previous problems encountered following the judgment in *London Borough of Lewisham v Malcolm* [2008] have been remedied through a new definition of discrimination based on disability in s 15 EA 2010:

A person (A) discriminates against a disabled person (B) if—

(1) A treats B unfavourably because of something arising in consequence of B's disability, and

(2) A cannot show that the treatment is a proportionate means of achieving a legitimate aim.

Subsection (1) does not apply if A shows that A did not know, and could not reasonably have been expected to know, that B had the disability.

Definition of disability

A person is disabled where he/she has a physical/mental impairment that has a substantial and long-tem adverse effect on his/her ability to carry out normal day-to-day activities.

Reasonable adjustments

An employer is required to make reasonable adjustments to his/her premises or procedures to ensure disabled employees are not put at a substantial disadvantage compared with non-disabled employees (s 212(1) of EA 2010). This includes recruitment and selection procedures for job applicants.

The EA 2010 identifies the following three-step procedure as being reasonable for compliance:

1 Avoid substantial disadvantage where a provision, criterion or practice applied by or on behalf of the employers puts the disabled person at such a substantial disadvantage when compared with persons without the disability (s 20(3));

2 Remove or alter an existing physical feature (or provide the means to avoid it) where it puts the disabled person at a substantial disadvantage compared with persons without the disability (s 20(4));

3 Provide an auxiliary aid/service where a disabled person would (but for this aid) be put at a substantial disadvantage compared with persons without the disability (s 20(5)).

The requirement is for the employer to make reasonable adjustments for 'actual' persons with a disability rather than hypothetical persons. As such, the requirement becomes effective where the employer knew, or should have reasonably known, of the existence of the disability, and where to take no action would likely have the effect of substantially disadvantaging the applicant to a job or an existing employee. (See *HJ Heinz Co Ltd v Kenrick* [2002] and *Ridout v TC Group* [1998]).

An employer's duty to make reasonable adjustments applies to enabling an employee to remain in work, it does not extend to provide compensation if an employee has to leave due to his/her ill-health (see *Tameside Hospital NHS Foundation Trust v Mylott* [2011]).

Comparator

The use of a comparator is the same for the other forms of direct discrimination. However, the comparator should be someone with the same disability as the claimant. There is no generic 'disabled person' for comparisons.

RELIGION OR BELIEF

Discrimination in employment on the grounds of religion or belief was made unlawful by the RRA 1976 and the Employment Equality (Religion or Belief) Regulations 2003 (SI 2003/1660) (which does not extend to political belief or discrimination for the absence of belief). It is now contained in s 10 of EA 2010, which provides for protection against discrimination on the basis of the person's religion or lack of religion, religious or philosophical belief, or his/her non-belief.

Protection against discrimination on the basis of this protected characteristic is afforded against direct and indirect forms of discrimination, against victimisation, and against harassment.

Genuine occupational requirement defence

An employer may seek to justify an otherwise directly discriminatory act where it is a genuine occupational requirement of the particular job. In relation to where an employer has an ethos based religion or belief, the employer can rely on this defence if it can be demonstrated that, in relation to that ethos and the nature of the work to be undertaken:

1 The requirement of possessing that particular region or belief is an occupational requirement;

2 The application of the requirement is a proportionate means of achieving a legitimate aim; and

3 The person (claimant) fails to meet the requirement or the employer possesses reasonable grounds to believe that he/she does not meet the requirement.

AGE DISCRIMINATION

The legislation came into effect on 1st October 2006 (Employment Equality (Age) Regulations 2006), as required under the EC Equal Treatment Framework Directive [2000/78].

The EA 2010 enables direct and indirect discrimination claims against employers in recruitment, promotion and training. Indeed, it should be noted that age is one of the protected characteristic that permits a justification of direct discrimination. Discrimination is permitted where the employer can successfully demonstrate that the less favourable treatment suffered by the claimant on the basis of his/her age is a proportionate means of achieving a legitimate aim. This is the 'objective justification test'.

The EAT has held that where an employer refers to an employee being 'too old to change' this may provide a basis to infer age discrimination (*Live Nations (Venues) UK Ltd v Hussain* [2008]).

GENDER REASSIGNMENT

Gender reassignment refers to a person who is proposing to undergo, is under going or has undergone a process (or part of a process) for the purpose of reassigning his/her sex by changing physiological or other attributes of sex (a transsexual person) (EA 2010 s 7). Permanency is required.

The EA 2010 protects a woman (for example) who wishes to live permanently as a man even though she does not intend to undergo any medical procedures. This differs from the previous legislative initiatives which required the claimant to be undergoing medical supervision.

The EA 2010 provides the individual with protection from discrimination on the basis of his/her protected characteristic. However, it does not extend to allowing the transsexual person to 'benefit' from his/her change in areas such as marriage, parenthood, social security benefits, succession, peerages, and sport. He/she will be recognised as being of the gender reassigned to, he/she will be issued with a new birth certificate, and be able to marry under the new gender.

PREGNANCY
To discriminate against a woman on the grounds of her pregnancy amounts to unlawful discrimination. The case law upholds the view that there is no need for the pregnant woman to compare herself with a hypothetical sick man: *Dekker v Stichting Vormingscentrum voor Jong Volwassenen (VJV – Centrum) Plus* [1992]; *Webb v EMO Air Cargo (UK) Ltd (No 2)* [1995], although the latter case suggests that this is restricted to non-fixed term contracts, whilst *Caruana v Manchester Airport plc* [1996] and the Court of Justice in *Jimenez Melgar* [2001] suggest that it applies equally to fixed term contracts.

> ▶ WEBB v EMO AIR CARGO (UK) LTD (NO 2) [1995]

Webb had been employed by EMO as replacement for a woman on maternity leave, with the intention of continuing the employment following the pregnant woman's return.

Shortly after her engagement, Webb discovered she was pregnant, and upon informing her employer of this, she was dismissed.

The House of Lords, following a reference to the Court of Justice, held that this was a breach of the SDA 1975 and direct sex discrimination, and no comparator was available or necessary. Dismissal on the grounds of pregnancy is automatically discriminatory and unfair dismissal.

It should be noted that:

- comparison with the sick man may, however, be appropriate once the maternity leave period is complete (*Handels-og Kontorfunktionaerernes Forbund i Danmark (acting for Hertz) v Dansk Arbejdsgiverforening (acting for Aldi Marked K/S)* [1991]);

- protection for the pregnant woman ceases at the end of the maternity leave period (*British Telecommunications plc v Roberts and Longstaffe* [1996]; *Handels-og Kontorfunktionaerernes Forbund i Danmark v Dansk Handel and Service (acting on behalf of Fotex Supermarked A/S)* [1997]);

- dismissal of a pregnant woman because of her pregnancy is automatically unfair and may constitute direct discrimination contrary to Art 5(1) of Directive 76/207 (*Brown v Rentokil Initial UK Ltd* [1998]) and the Employment Rights Act 1996.

The EA 2010 provides specific protection for pregnant employees, such as the right not to be dismissed, the right to attend doctor's appointments, the right not be treated less favourably because of pregnancy or maternity leave (s 18) and so on. Section 55(1) of ERA 1996 specifically enables a pregnant employee to have paid time off work to attend the appointment – insofar as it was made on the advice of a doctor, registered midwife, or registered health worker.

The protection of women due to their protected characteristic of pregnancy or maternity leave begins when the woman becomes pregnant. It continues until the end of her maternity leave or until she returns to work (if this is earlier) (s 18(6)). Outside of these times, unfavourable treatment because of her pregnancy would be considered sex discrimination rather than pregnancy and maternity discrimination (s 18(7)).

FORMS OF DISCRIMINATION – PROHIBITED CONDUCT

Discriminatory behaviour is identified as prohibited conduct (covered in ss 13–27). The EA 2010 harmonised the definitions of prohibited conduct as applicable to the protected characteristics.

DIRECT DISCRIMINATION

Direct discrimination applies to all of the protected characteristics.

It occurs when a person treats another less favourably because of a protected characteristic than he/she would of a person without the characteristic. A person is treated less favourably than another due to:

(a) a protected characteristic he/she possesses; or

(b) a protected characteristic it is thought he/she possesses (this amounts to perceptive discrimination); or

(c) his/her association with someone who has a protected characteristic (this amounts to associative discrimination) (s 13).

As such, perceptive and associative forms of discrimination are included in the Act.

■ the test for establishing direct discrimination, laid down in *R v Birmingham CC ex p EOC* [1989] and confirmed in *James v Eastleigh BC* [1990] is:

- was there an act of discrimination?
- but for the applicant's protected characteristic would he or she have been treated differently (that is, more favourably)?

❯ JAMES v EASTLEIGH BC [1990]

This case involved Mr James and his wife's use of a local authority swimming pool. Pensioners were entitled to free access, which Mrs James had as she was 61, but as the national retirement age for men was 65, and Mr James was also 61, he was not entitled to the same access.

The House of Lords, in using the test noted above, found the different retirement ages discriminatory (with the subsequent levelling of the ages at 65 for men and women).

If both questions are answered in the affirmative, direct discrimination is established. Motive is irrelevant: *Grieg v Community Industry* [1979], although a Genuine Occupational Requirement defence exists. The conduct of the hypothetical employer is not the basis of the test for direct discrimination: *Zafar v Glasgow CC* [1998]. Therefore, the 'range of reasonable responses' test used in unfair dismissal is not applicable in discrimination cases.

❯ GRIEG v COMMUNITY INDUSTRY [1979]

Miss Grieg, along with another woman, was due to join the company's painting and decorating team. However, as the other woman did not report for work, and there had been problems where only one woman had been part of the team, to protect Grieg, she was not hired.

The EAT held that this was a clear case of direct sex discrimination, and the good intentions/motives of the employer were irrelevant to this determination.

In relation to the protected characteristic of pregnancy and maternity, the test is not 'less favourable' treatment, but 'unfavourable' treatment as there is no need for a comparison with other workers.

Discriminatory job advertisements are held to amount to direct discrimination, and following the Court of Justice's decision in *Centrum voor gelijkheid van kansen en voor racismebestrijding v Firma Feryn* [2008], claims may be brought by individuals rather than bodies such as the Commission for Equality and Human Rights (overturning *Cardiff Women's Aid v Hartup* [1984]).

■ Following the EA 2010, it is possible for an employer to treat a person with the protected characteristic of age less favourably insofar as the employer can justify this as a proportionate means of achieving a legitimate aim.

■ A disabled person may be treated more favourably than an employer treats a non-disabled person.

ASSOCIATIVE DISCRIMINATION

A person may face discrimination due to his/her association with another person who has a protected characteristic (where he/she does not personally possess the protected characteristic). As such, where the discrimination is due to the individual's association with a person with the protected characteristic or it is transferred, protection is granted. This is broadly similar to the protection granted under the RRA 1976. For example, in *Showboat Entertainment Centre Ltd v Owens* [1984], Owens, who was white, was dismissed from his job as the manager of an amusement centre for failing to obey an order to exclude black people. Unlawful discrimination was held to have taken place. See also *Weatherfield Ltd t/a Van and Truck Rentals v Sargent* [1999].

Protection applies to the protected characteristics of race; religion and belief; and sexual orientation as was under the previous legislation. The protected characteristics of age; disability; sex and gender reassignment are newly protected under the EA 2010. However, marriage and civil partnership and pregnancy and maternity are not protected by the provision.

PERCEPTIVE DISCRIMINATION

The EA 2010 protects against a person being directly discrimination against on the basis that those persons performing the discriminatory acts have done so believing the victim possesses a protected characteristic. Hence, this form of discrimination is actionable where the victim does not actually posses the characteristic.

The protected characteristics of age; race; religion or belief; and sexual orientation continued to be protected as they were under previous legislation. Disability, gender reassignment and sex are newly covered by the EA 2010. Both marriage and civil partnership and pregnancy and maternity are not protected.

HARASSMENT

Harassment is defined in s 26 EA 2010 as:

(1) A person (A) harasses another (B) if —
  (a) A engages in unwanted conduct related to a relevant protected characteristic, and
  (b) the conduct has the purpose or effect of —
    (i) violating B's dignity, or
    (ii) creating an intimidating, hostile, degrading, humiliating or offensive environment for B.

(2) A also harasses B if —
  (a) A engages in unwanted conduct of a sexual nature, and
  (b) the conduct has the purpose or effect referred to in subsection (1)(b).

(3) A also harasses B if —
  (a) A or another person engages in unwanted conduct of a sexual nature or that is related to gender reassignment or sex,
  (b) the conduct has the purpose or effect referred to in subsection (1)(b), and
  (c) because of B's rejection of or submission to the conduct, A treats B less favourably than A would treat B if B had not rejected or submitted to the conduct.

Therefore, the EA 2010 protects against harassment related to a person of a relevant protected characteristic; sexual harassment; and less favourable treatment of a worker because of the sexual harassment or harassment related to sex or gender reassignment.

Importantly, the EA 2010 protects against harassment due to perception or association with someone with a protected characteristic.

The wording of 'purpose or effect' is important as they enable a claim for harassment even where this was not the intended effect of the harasser. For example, male workers may download an image of a naked woman at work which they may find amusing. A female colleague (for instance) may know this is happening and as a result may feel it is an action creating a hostile and humiliating environment. This would establish an actionable case for harassment unless the victim can be shown to be hypersensitive. Key issues in harassment are the perception of the victim (a subjective test); his/her personal circumstances (such as health, culture and so on); and whether it was reasonable that the conduct would have that effect on the worker (an objective test).

One of the more interesting aspects of the developments brought about with the EA 2010 has been an employer's potential liability for the actions of third parties (such as customers/clients of the employer rather than contractors or persons under the control of the employer). An employer will be liable for harassment undertaken by a third party where it has occurred on at least two previous occasions (although not necessarily by the same person), and the employer was aware (or should reasonably have been aware) of the harassment and failed to take reasonable steps to prevent its occurrence.

Despite the word harassment meaning a series of actions, a single act of a serious nature will support a claim of harassment:

> ▶ BRACEBRIDGE ENGINEERING LTD v DARBY [1990]
>
> Darby resigned due to a failure on the part of her employer to take action on her allegation of sexual assault by two colleagues.
>
> The tribunal and the EAT each held that this single, serious act could constitute a detriment as required under the SDA 1975, notwithstanding the textual definition of detriment being a sustained 'course of action'.

A single verbal comment, if sufficiently serious, may amount to harassment: *Insitu Cleaning v Heads* [1995].

The complainant must also show that he/she has suffered a detriment when claiming sexual harassment. This may have an impact on the amount of compensation awarded: *Snowball v Gardner Merchant Ltd* [1987]; *Wileman v Minilec Engineering Ltd* [1988].

> ▶ WILEMAN v MINILEC ENGINEERING LTD [1988]
>
> This case involved a woman who claimed she had been a victim of verbal and physical sexual harassment by the director of the company.

> Part of the defence of the employer was that Wileman was in the habit of wearing scanty clothing and 'flaunting' herself.
>
> The EAT held that she had been the victim of discrimination, but as this had not adversely affected her (after the first hearing she had appeared dressed scantily for a national newspaper) she was awarded nominal damages of £50.

Intentional harassment is a criminal offence: s 4A of the Criminal Justice and Public Order Act 1994.

Protection from Harassment Act 1997, a criminal statute, also allows the complainant to bring a civil action against the harasser. Harassment, in this case, is defined as being a course of conduct that amounts to harassment of another and which the perpetrator knows, or ought to know, amounts to harassment. There must have been at least two instances of harassment, although verbal harassment is included. Damages and/or an injunction may be awarded.

Conduct will be regarded as having the effect mentioned in this section of the EA 2010 if, having regard to all the circumstances, including the perception of the victim, that it should reasonably be considered as having that effect.

INDIRECT DISCRIMINATION

The prohibited conduct of indirect discrimination has been provided with a common definition applicable to the protected characteristics. Note from the outset that each of the protected characteristics with the exception of marriage and civil partnership and pregnancy and maternity are covered. (A claim of indirect SEX discrimination may be available in cases involving pregnancy and maternity.) The legislation is aimed at a provision, criterion or practice which, on the surface, appears to be seemingly neutral or innocuous, rather than discriminatory, but which, in effect, particularly affects people who share a protected characteristic and it puts them (or would put them) at a particular disadvantage.

Indirect discrimination may be justified where the measure is 'a proportionate means of achieving a legitimate aim' (s 19 of EA 2010). The wording 'or would put them' enables a challenge to a provision, criterion or practice which has not yet been applied but whose affect would be discriminatory if it were. Hence there is a two-stage test to be applied. (1) is the aim legitimate? and if yes (2) is it necessary in the particular circumstances as being proportionate?

Provision, criterion or practice
The tribunal will assess the employer's provision, criterion, or practice in an objective manner to assess whether there may be a justification for its imposition.

The objective nature of the examination considers any tangible grounds (not what an employer believes) that would make such a provision acceptable. The test considers the *prima facie* evidence of discrimination presented by the claimant and if this is satisfied, the next stage is to demonstrate that it has caused the claimant a disadvantage.

Examples of a *prima facie* case of unlawful discrimination (developed under the old laws) include:

■ a full time post (*Home Office v Holmes* [1984]);

■ a mobility clause (*Meade-Hill and National Union of Civil and Public Servants v British Council* [1995]);

■ a language qualification (*Perera v Civil Service Commission* [1983]);

■ insistence on working from an office (*Lockwood v Crawley Warren Group Ltd* [2000]).

A disadvantage
The claimant must show that he/she has suffered a disadvantage through the application of the provision, criterion or practice, or that he/she would be disadvantaged if it were used.

The test used to be based on pure statistical evidence demonstrating a 'considerably smaller proportion' of (for example) women could comply than men (see *University of Manchester v Jones* [1993]). Whilst this method will remain relevant in certain circumstances, the law was broadened to include evidence provided by experts or other witnesses.

Examples of how a particular disadvantage will be demonstrated include:

- the numbers of women and men who can comply with the provision if the disparity is large (significant) (see *London Underground Ltd v Edwards (No 2)* [1998]; *Chief Constable of Avon v Chew* [2002]);

- a small difference in the percentages of who can comply may be relevant if this is a constant over a longer time period;

- evidence is presented to the tribunal that, on the facts, suggests that the disparity is due to the protected characteristic.

The disadvantage is taken from a practical point of view: *Price v Civil Service Commission* [1978].

Places the claimant at a disadvantage
This provides the complainant with *locus standi* and establishes that a loss has been incurred: *Home Office v Holmes* [1984].

Proportionate means of achieving a legitimate aim
Once the claimant has presented his/her evidence establishing a *prima facie* case, the employer is under an obligation to demonstrate the provision, criterion or practice was a proportionate means of achieving a legitimate aim.

The Court of Justice in *Bilka-Kaufhaus GmbH v Weber von Hartz* [1987] established guidelines as to what would justify a proportionate provision. In English law the Court of Appeal (*R (on the application of Elias) v Secretary of State for Defence* [2006]) stated that in assessing whether the provision, criterion or practice is proportionate the following questions should be asked:

- Is the objective to be achieved sufficiently important to justify limiting a right provided by the law?

- Is the measure(s) taken by the employer connected to the objective to be achieved?

- Is the measure(s) no more onerous than is required to accomplish the objective?

Justification
The onus now moves to the employer to show that the provision, criterion or practice is justifiable, irrespective of the protected characteristic of the person to whom it is applied. Generalisations will not succeed.

The test of justifiability requires an objective balance between the discriminatory effect of the condition and the reasonable needs of the party who applies the condition: *Hampson v Department of Education and Science* [1989]. The condition must be necessary and appropriate.

> ◗ HAMPSON v DEPARTMENT OF EDUCATION AND SCIENCE [1989]
>
> Hampson was from Hong Kong and applied for qualified teacher status in the UK.
>
> This was a power of the Secretary of State for Education who refused the application as her training was not comparable with that in the UK, and that under s 41 of RRA 1976, there was protection from this potentially discriminatory act if carried out in pursuance of an enactment or power given to the Minister under delegated legislation.
>
> The House of Lords held that this power was specific to the wording of the Act and was not a requirement, and hence the decision was unlawful.

In *Cherfi v G4S Security Services Ltd* [2011] the EAT, following its earlier decision in *Woodcock v Cumbria Primary Care NHS Trust* [2010], held (albeit *obiter*) that an employer may rely on cost issues alone to justify an indirectly discriminatory measure. Here, a Muslim man employed as a security guard, regularly left work on Friday to attend a Mosque. This left the employer with fewer guards than it was contractually obliged to provide. When the employer stopped the attendance at the Mosque the claimant brought an action for indirect religious discrimination on the basis that the employer's policy put Muslims at a particular disadvantage. However, the EAT ruled that the financial implications of the employer being in breach of contract justified the imposition of the provision.

VICTIMISATION

An individual who suffers a detriment because he/she performed a 'protected act'; the employer believes he/she has done so, or that he/she will perform a protected act in the future (s 27(1) of EA 2010) has a complaint for victimisation.

A protected act includes:

■ Initiating proceedings under the EA 2010 (s 27(2)(a));

■ Providing evidence/information in relation to proceedings under the EA 2010 (s 27(2)(b));

■ Doing anything related to the provisions of the EA 2010 (s 27(2)(c));

■ Making an allegation that another person has done something in contravention of the EA 2010 (s 27(2)(d)); or

■ Making/trying to obtain a 'relevant pay disclosure' from a colleague/former colleague (s 77(3).

There is no requirement for the claimant to use a comparator in a claim of victimisation. Where a complaint is made maliciously, or the employee supports a complaint he/she knows is untrue, protection afforded under the EA 2010 is lost (s 27(3)).

> ### ❱ ST HELEN'S BOROUGH COUNCIL v DERBYSHIRE AND OTHERS [2007]
>
> Here a group of workers, employed by the Council as catering staff, sought to initiate a claim for work of equal value with male road sweepers. Some claims of the group were settled but others proceeded to a hearing, with the case finally being heard by the House of Lords.
>
> The Council, prior to the tribunal hearing, sent the claimants letters informing them if the Council lost the case, then the provision of school meals may be discontinued and, consequently, jobs lost.
>
> The Lords considered this went beyond the reasonable protection of the Council's interests and instead was a tool to intimidate the claimants to stop their action. This was a case of victimisation.

There has to be a link between the protected act and the less favourable treatment.

The rule against victimisation applies both during and after employment (such as refusing to provide a reference): (*Coote v Granada Hospitality Ltd* [1998]).

Also, if a reference is provided by ex-employers, care has to be taken to ensure it is not discriminatory: *Chief Constable of West Yorkshire Police v Khan* [2001].

Employment

The complainant must establish that he has been discriminated against, either in respect of employment or in relation to the provision of goods, facilities and services, education, etc. In the employment field, this covers the arrangements for selection for employment (for example, when a job offer is withdrawn when the employers discover that the employee-to-be is pregnant), terms on which employment is offered, or the refusal or omission to offer employment. It also covers discrimination during the employment relationship, that is, access or refusal of access to opportunities for promotion, transfer or training, as well as the termination of employment or subjecting the complainant to any other detriment.

Exceptions to direct discrimination – genuine occupational qualifications

There is (in most instances applicable to the protected characteristics) no justification for direct sex discrimination. However, there exist exceptions (and genuine occupational qualifications), some of which are common sense, others are necessary due to the nature of the employment. Genuine occupational qualifications include (Sch 9 of EA 2010):

- Where the essential nature of the job calls for a man for reasons of physiology (excluding physical strength or stamina); or in dramatic performances; or for authenticity;

- The job needs to be held by a man to preserve decency or privacy;

- The nature or location of the establishment makes it impracticable for the holder of the job to live elsewhere than in the premises provided by the employer; and separate living accommodation/sanitary facilities for women are unavailable. Note, where the employer simply does not wish to make an adaptation, and this would be reasonable to do so, the defence will not be accepted (*Wallace v Peninsular and Oriental Steam Navigation Company* [1979]);

- The holder of the job provides individuals with personal services promoting their welfare or education (or similar services) that can be most effectively provided by a man (see *Tottenham Green Under Fives Centre v Marshall (No. 2)* [1991]);

■ The job is required to be held by a man because it is likely to involve the performance of the duties outside the UK in a country whose laws/customs mean that the job could not, or could not effectively, be performed by a woman;

■ The job involves participation as an artist's or photographic model in the production of a work of art, in which a person of that racial group is required for authenticity.

It is not a genuine occupational qualification to employ only women in a female dress shop (*Etam plc v Rowan* [1989]) or only men in a men's clothing shop (*Wylie v Dee and Co (Menswear) Ltd* [1978]). If, at the time of the complaint, there are no employees because the business has not begun to operate, the genuine occupational qualification defence may still operate: *Lasertop Ltd v Webster* [1997].

VICARIOUS LIABILITY OF THE EMPLOYER

Employers are vicariously liable for discriminatory acts – including harassment – carried out by their employees and third parties (reversing *MacDonald v Advocate General for Scotland* [2003]), unless the employer can show that he/she took all reasonable steps to prevent the occurrence of the act. The test for vicarious liability is generally somewhat stricter than the common law test: *Tower Boot Co Ltd v Jones* [1997]. This is to prevent the employer from success-fully claiming that the employee was acting outside the course of his employment (the 'We don't pay him to do that' argument) when he carried out the act. For example, in *Tower Boot*, the complainant had been subjected to racist name calling, branding with a hot screwdriver and whipping. The Court of Appeal held that to allow the employer to succeed in his claim that the employees were acting outside the course of their employment would allow an employer to escape liability and lead to an increase in acts of harassment.

An employer may avoid a claim under of vicarious liability if he/she took 'reasonable steps' to prevent the discrimination. The 'three-strikes' rule applies and on the third strike where performed by a third party, where the employer has not taken reasonable steps to prevent the harassment, it becomes actionable. Reasonable steps must involve some practical action and then the tribunal will consider whether these were reasonably practicable in the circumstances (*Canniffe v East Yorkshire Council* [2000]).

The Court of Appeal held that steps that require expense, the time of the parties and putting them to significant trouble, and those that may be counterproductive, will not amount to reasonable steps if, on assessment, they would likely achieve nothing:

> ### ▶ CROFT v ROYAL MAIL GROUP PLC [2003]
>
> Croft was a former employee of the company who claimed under the SDA against treatment she felt amounted to direct sex discrimination.
>
> Croft was a male who was undergoing gender reassignment, and during a period called 'real life test' Croft was required to use a unisex toilet rather than a male or female facility.
>
> The Court of Appeal held that this was fair as it would only have been required during this real life test until the reassignment was complete. Other steps taken could have been counter-productive and would have amounted to nothing.

COMPENSATION

The principal remedy for discrimination is compensation, but tribunals may also make a declaration and issue a recommendation that the employer removes the discrimination.

There is no statutory limit on the amount of compensation awarded (cf claims for unfair dismissal). Interest is payable on compensation: *Marshall v Southampton and South West Hampshire AHA (Teaching) (No 2)* [1993].

Note the following:

■ All awards for compensation should include a sum for injury to feelings (*Sharifi v Strathclyde Regional Council* [1992]; *Armitage, Marsden and HM Prison Service v Johnson* [1997]; *O'Donoghue v Redcar Borough Council* [2001]).

- Claims for discrimination can include claims for damages for personal injury, including psychiatric harm (*Sheriff v Klyne Tugs (Lowestoft) Ltd* [1999]; *HM Prison Service v Salmon* [2001]).

- Aggravated damages may be awarded (see *Alexander v Home Office* [1988]). Exemplary damages are not available in discrimination cases (*Ministry of Defence v Meredith* [1995]).

- There is a three-month time limit from the date of the last alleged act for bringing claims.

THE EMPLOYMENT RELATIONS ACT 1999 AND THE EMPLOYMENT ACT 2002

The Employment Relations Act introduced a right to unpaid leave for parents to care for children under five years born after 18 December 1999. It also provided a right to take unpaid leave to cope with domestic emergencies concerning dependants. The Employment Act 2002 provides for further maternity and paternity rights, including time off for adoptive parents.

People who have worked for their employer for one year have the right to unpaid parental leave (up to 13 weeks' unpaid leave before your child is five). Where the child has a disability, the period of leave is extended to 18 weeks' leave which must be taken before the child is 18.

Further protection is afforded to fathers. The Additional Paternity Leave Regulations 2010, which were in force from 6th April 2010 but only really apply to children born (or adopted) on or after 3rd April 2011, provide that additional paternity leave will be available for a minimum of two weeks, and a maximum of 26 weeks; it must not start until at least 20 weeks after the birth (or placement in relation to adoption); it must end not later than 12 months after the birth (or placement); and it must be taken in complete weeks. The leave will be applicable where the mother has returned to work and therefore this may prevent the discrimination experienced by women of childbearing age. Here, the mother and father can arrange to share the paid leave between them (insofar as the leave is taken by the father in the mother's 39 week maternity pay period).

You should now be confident that you would be able to tick all the boxes on the checklist at the beginning of this chapter. To check your knowledge of Discrimination why not visit the companion website and take the Multiple Choice Question test. Check your understanding of the terms and vocabulary used in this chapter with the flashcard glossary.

Termination of employment

4

Dismissals with the required notice are fair at common law for any reason

In the absence of a contractual term, statute provides a minimum of one week's notice (after one month and up to two years' employment) and thereafter one weeks' notice for each year worked (to a maximum of 12 weeks)

Payments in lieu of notice have to be expressly included in the contract

Dismissal without notice is generally held to be a breach of contract

Dismissal without notice (summary dismissal) can be justified in the event of the worker committing a fundamental breach of the contract

The doctrine of frustration ends the contract if the unforeseen event was neither party's fault

A fundamental breach of the contract will allow the employee to accept this as a repudiation and claim constructive dismissal (a form of unfair dismissal)

Evidence discovered after the dismissal is admitted by the courts and may be used to make lawful an otherwise wrongful dismissal

The primary remedy in wrongful dismissal claims is damages, although injunctions are used to protect the parties' interests

TERMINATIONS INVOLVING DISMISSAL AT COMMON LAW

DISMISSAL WITH NOTICE

The parties should expressly agree the applicable length of notice. If this period is greater than the statutory minimum, the worker is entitled to rely on the more beneficial term.

If no notice is expressly agreed, the common law requires that 'reasonable notice' should be given, with the length depending on such factors as the seniority and status of the employee. In *Hill v Parsons* [1972] the Court of Appeal held that the employee, who had been engaged with the company for 35 years, was entitled to 6 months (or even 12 months) notice even though the statutory provision granted him only three months.

Apart from any contractual provision for notice, an employee is entitled to a statutory minimum period of notice. The employer must give one weeks' notice to an employee who has between one month and two years' continuous service, and then not less than one week's notice for each further year of continuous service, up to a maximum of 12 years. In return, the employee must give at least one weeks' notice of resignation if employed for more than a month (s 86 of the ERA 1996).

Insofar as the correct notice period is provided, or payment in lieu of notice (where allowed through the contract), the individual has no claim for breach, and the employer may use any reason to dismiss. In order for a payment in lieu of notice to be used, the contract must expressly state that this is available and it will not be implied into the contract (*Morrish v NTL Group* [2007]).

DISMISSAL FOR BREACH OF A FUNDAMENTAL TERM

The conduct of the individual may be viewed as being sufficiently serious to justify immediate termination of employment without notice. In this event, the individual will lose entitlement to both contractual and statutory minimum notice. Examples include wilful disobedience of a lawful order, theft of or wilful damage to the employer's property, violence at work, dishonesty, etc. Where an individual has fundamentally undermined the trust and confidence between the parties, an employer is entitled to accept the repudiation and terminate the contract (*Dunn v AAH Ltd* [2010]).

The most common form of dismissal of an individual is for gross misconduct or gross negligence.

The 'gross' element of the action relates to a serious breach of the contract which the employer is entitled to accept as a repudiation of the contract.

Less serious actions may amount to dismissal due to the individual's conduct that has continued over a period of time.

An employer should clearly establish action likely to be considered gross misconduct.

The ACAS Code of Practice on Disciplinary and Grievance Procedures provides examples of what constitutes gross misconduct that may be relevant in wrongful dismissal cases

WRONGFUL DISMISSAL

This is defined as dismissal with no or insufficient notice where the employer cannot justify its failure to give (sufficient) notice. The remedy is damages, which is assessed on contractual principles. For example, damages run only until the end of the notice period and the doctrine of mitigation applies. As far as remedies for dismissal are concerned, the following weaknesses have been identified:

■ The low level of damages awarded to successful litigants, generally only compensating for the appropriate notice period which should have been given: see *Addis v Gramophone Co Ltd* [1909]; *Bliss v SE Thames RHA* [1985]. For example, damages cannot be awarded to compensate for the stress of losing a job, injured feelings or the manner of dismissal. More recently, however, the House of Lords has partly sidestepped the long established approach in *Addis*. In *Malik v BCCI SA (In Liq)* [1997], their Lordships allowed 'stigma' damages to be recovered by ex-employees of BCCI in respect of injury to their reputations allegedly caused by the bank conducting a dishonest and corrupt business – however, their Lordships made clear that the decision should be confined to the particular facts of the case; see *Johnson v Unisys Ltd* [1999].

▶ MALIK v BCCI SA (IN LIQ) [1997]

The case involved employees of the disgraced bank (BCCI) who sought to recover damages to the injury they suffered to their reputation, and consequent problems in finding new employment. This was due to BCCI conducting a dishonest business.

The House of Lords held that the bank was under an implied obligation not to run a dishonest business that damaged the mutual trust and confidence between the parties.

■ The lack of procedural protection for most employees, with only so called office holders and those whose employment has 'statutory underpinnings' being entitled to the remedies of public law (see *Ridge v Baldwin* [1964]). Attempts to broaden the range of workers in the public sector who could apply for judicial review as an alternative remedy to unfair dismissal have been strongly resisted by the courts. It has been held that, where the dispute involves private rights arising out of the contract of employment, as opposed to public rights, then judicial review is inappropriate (see *R v Berkshire HA ex p Walsh* [1984]).

■ The inability of dismissed employees to regain their jobs because of the general rule against ordering specific performance of contracts – although this rule has been relaxed and injunctions restraining dismissals and breaches of contract by employers have been granted where the court has been satisfied that trust and confidence remained between the parties (see *Irani v South West Hampshire HA* [1985]; *Powell v London Borough of Brent* [1987]; *Hughes v London Borough of Southwark* [1988]; *Boyo v Lambeth Borough Council* [1995]; *Anderson v Pringle of Scotland Ltd* [1998]).

▶ ANDERSON v PRINGLE OF SCOTLAND LTD [1998]

The company had entered into a collective agreement with the GMB trade union over selection procedures for redundancy that had been implied into Anderson's contract.

Redundancies were to be made on the basis of 'last in, first out' but Pringle, in 1997, wished to make 290 employees redundant and made the selections not on the basis of the agreement with the trade union. Anderson was one of the employees selected, and would not have been had the agreed procedures been used.

The Court of Session (the Scottish equivalent of the Court of Appeal) allowed an injunction to prevent the redundancy as the agreement had become a term of the contract, and, as the trust and confidence between the parties had not been breached, this was an appropriate remedy.

TERMINATIONS NOT INVOLVING DISMISSAL AT COMMON LAW

DEATH OR DISSOLUTION OF THE EMPLOYER
But see below.

FRUSTRATION
'Frustration' is a legal concept that, if it applies, brings the employment contract automatically to an end, without resulting in a dismissal. As a result, there is no liability to continue paying wages or to pay compensation for unfair dismissal, redundancy, etc.

In order for the doctrine of frustration to apply, two essential factors must be present:

■ there must be some event, not foreseen or provided for by the parties to the contract at the time it was made, which either makes it impossible for the contract to be performed at all or at least renders its performance radically different from that which the parties envisaged when they made the contract; and

■ the event must have occurred without the fault of either contracting party. Frustration will not operate if it was 'self-induced' or caused by the fault of a party.

Events that have been held to frustrate the contract include:

■ the conscription of the employee to national service;

■ internment as an enemy alien during wartime.

However, frustration arguments have been most frequently employed in the case of long-term absence through sickness or imprisonment.

Where absence is due to sickness, a number of factors will generally be relevant in deciding whether a contract is frustrated. These include:

■ the terms of the contract, including any provision for sick pay;

■ how long the employment would be likely to last in the absence of sickness;

■ whether the employee holds a 'key position';

■ the nature of the illness and how long it has already continued, and the prospects of recovery;

■ the period of past employment.

> ### ▶ CONDOR v THE BARRON KNIGHTS LTD [1966]

Condor was a drummer for the band the Barron Knights. He was 16 years old when he joined, contracted for five years and was to perform for seven nights a week. Soon the pressure became too much and he suffered a mental disorder, which doctors said would lead to a mental breakdown if he continued with the present work-load. The band considered that Condor could not complete the contract and terminated the agreement, and Condor claimed wrongful dismissal.

It was held that as Condor could no longer fulfil the contract, he was permanently ill and the contract was frustrated.

The leading cases from which this test is derived are: *Marshall v Harland and Wolff Ltd* [1972]; *Egg Stores (Stamford Hill) Ltd v Leibovici* [1977]; *Hart v AR Marshall & Sons (Bulwell) Ltd* [1977]; and *Notcutt v Universal Equipment Co Ltd* [1986].

In *Williams v Watsons Luxury Coaches Ltd* [1990], Wood J warned against too 'easy' an application of the doctrine; otherwise, there would be no scope for the doctrine of dismissal, with the effect that no remedy could be awarded for wrongful dismissal, unfair dismissal or on redundancy.

In the past, imprisonment was thought to be 'self-induced' frustration. However, the Court of Appeal ruled that a custodial sentence of six months does have the effect of frustrating the contract. It was felt that it was the sentence passed by the trial judge – as opposed to the employee's criminal conduct – which was the frustrating event. Consequently, this was not a case of self-induced frustration: *FC Shepherd & Co Ltd v Jerrom* [1986].

EXPIRY OF A FIXED/LIMITED TERM CONTRACT
The expiry of a fixed term contract does not constitute a dismissal at common law, but it is deemed to be a dismissal by statute (see below).

TERMINATION BY MUTUAL AGREEMENT
As with other contracts, a contract of employment may be terminated by the mutual consent of the parties. If the courts were to accept too readily that the contractual relationship had ended in this way, then access to employment protection would be severely threatened. In general, courts and tribunals have been reluctant to accept the argument that an employee has, in reality, agreed to give up his job and to forgo the possibility of an unfair dismissal or redundancy claim. The general principle applied by the courts is that if the sole cause of the employee's willingness to agree to resign is the threat of dismissal, he/she will be taken to have been dismissed (see *Sheffield v Oxford Controls Ltd* [1979]). If, however, other additional factors, such as financial inducements, affected the decision, it will be held that there was termination by mutual agreement: *Logan Salton v Durham CC* [1989]; *Birch v University of Liverpool* [1985]. The question to be answered is: who really terminated the contract (*Martin v MBS Fastenings (Glynwed) Distribution Ltd* [1983])?

> ▶ MARTIN v MBS FASTENINGS (GLYNWED) DISTRIBUTION LTD [1983]
>
> Here an employee was involved in an accident that resulted in one of the company's vehicles being badly damaged.

An investigation was planned and Martin was told it was likely to lead to his dismissal, therefore it was suggested that it would be in his interests to resign. Martin did resign but then claimed unfair dismissal as he had no choice in his actions.

The Court of Appeal held that as the tribunal had determined on the facts that his resignation was not a dismissal, then appeal courts had no right to overturn this finding.

An agreement for the automatic termination of a contract of employment on the occurrence of a certain event may be void under s 203(1) of the ERA 1996 (*Igbo v Johnson Matthey Chemicals Ltd* [1986]).

TERMINATIONS DEEMED TO BE DISMISSALS UNDER THE EMPLOYMENT RIGHTS ACT 1996

DEATH OR DISSOLUTION OF THE EMPLOYER

An act of the employer or any event affecting the employer (including death, dissolution of a partnership or winding up of a company) which has the effect of automatically terminating the contract at common law will be deemed to be dismissal for the purposes of redundancy, but not for an unfair dismissal claim: s 136(5) of the ERA 1996.

TERMINATION OF A CONTRACT BY THE EMPLOYER WITH OR WITHOUT NOTICE

See ss 95(1)(a) and 136(1)(a) of the ERA 1996.

AMBIGUOUS/UNAMBIGUOUS WORDS OF DISMISSAL/RESIGNATION

The legal principles in this area may be summarised as follows:

- if, taking into account the context in which they were uttered, the words unambiguously amount to a dismissal (or resignation), then this should be the finding of the tribunal (see *Sothern v Franks Charlesly & Co* [1981]);

- where, however, the words employed are ambiguous because they were uttered in the heat of the moment, the effect of the statement is determined by an objective test, that is, whether any 'reasonable' employer or employee might have understood the words to be tantamount to a dismissal or resignation (*BG Gale Ltd v Gilbert* [1978]);

■ A dismissal or resignation given in the heat of the moment may generally be withdrawn. However, the change of mind must not be so late that it is impossible to recover the words' effect (*Martin v Yeoman Aggregates Ltd* [1983]), nor, presumably, must the words used etc be sufficient to breach mutual trust and confidence.

▶ BG GALE LTD v GILBERT [1978]

Here a long-standing employee who was prone to temper informed his employer of his wish to resign by saying 'I am leaving ... I want my cards.' The employer accepted this resignation but subsequently the employee brought an unfair dismissal claim on the basis that his employer should not have taken his statement and actions as an actual resignation.

The Employment Appeal Tribunal (EAT) held that due to the unequivocal nature of the employee's statement, it was irrelevant to consider how a reasonable employer would have acted.

The Court of Appeal considered these principles in *Sovereign House Security Services Ltd v Savage* [1989]. It confirmed that an employment tribunal is entitled to look behind what was said unambiguously and find that, in the context or circumstances (such as a decision taken in the heat of the moment or by an immature employee), there was no real termination, despite appearances (see also *Kwik-Fit v Lineham* [1992]).

FAILURE TO RENEW A FIXED/LIMITED TERM CONTRACT
See ss 95(1)(b) and 136(1)(b) of the ERA 1996.

The expiry of a fixed term contract is deemed by statute to be a dismissal. It must have a definite starting and finishing date, although there may be provision for earlier termination by notice within the fixed term period: *BBC v Dixon* [1979].

Following the Fixed Term Employees (Prevention of Less Favourable Treatment) Regulations 2002, where an employee has been continuously employed under fixed term contracts for more than four years, and where the use of such fixed term contracts could not be objectively justified, the employee is taken to be permanently employed.

Where an employee is employed on a fixed term contract for more than two years, it was in the past possible for such an employee to agree in writing to waive any right to a redundancy payment; however, following the Fixed Term Employees (Prevention of Less Favourable Treatment) Regulations 2002 (above) it is no longer possible for employers to require this of their employees.

Note the distinction between fixed term contracts, on the one hand, and contracts to perform specific tasks or terminable on the occurrence of a specific event, on the other. In the latter category of cases, it has been held that there is no dismissal when the task is completed or the contingent event occurs: *Brown v Knowsley BC* [1986]. It should, however, also be noted that for the purpose of the Fixed Term Employees (Prevention of Less Favourable Treatment) Regulations 2002, both types of contract are taken to be 'fixed term contracts'.

CONSTRUCTIVE DISMISSAL

Where the employee terminates the contract, with or without notice, by reason of the employer's conduct that amounts to a fundamental breach of contract, this will be 'constructive dismissal': ss 95(1)(c) and 136(1)(c) of the ERA 1996. The leading case is *Western Excavating v Sharp* [1978].

> ▶ WESTERN EXCAVATING v SHARP [1978]
>
> Sharp had been suspended from work for five days without pay following his taking leave contrary to instructions from his employer. As he was short of money, Sharp requested an advance of his holiday pay, and subsequently a loan from the employer, who refused both requests.
>
> Sharp claimed this was a fundamental breach by the employer enabling him to resign and treat the refusal as an unfair dismissal.

> The Court of Appeal held that there was no requirement for the employer to acquiesce to the claim, neither had the employer breached any implied or express term of the contract. As such, there was no dismissal and therefore no right to claim unfair dismissal.

The elements of the concept are:

- Has the employer broken a term of the contract or made it clear that he does not intend to be bound by the contract?

- If yes, is the term which has or will be broken an essential or fundamental term of the contract?

- If yes, has the employee terminated the contract with or without notice in response to the breach within a reasonable time?

Employees who have been unfairly dismissed are entitled to compensation for all of their notice period – even where they may have secured alternative employment during this period/failed to mitigate their losses (*Norton Tool v Tewson* [1972]). This ruling had been extended to cases of constructive dismissal (*Stuart Peters v Bell* [2009]) but the Court of Appeal overturned the EAT's decision in *Stuart Peters v Bell*. Hence the position now is that the *Norton Tool* principle does NOT apply to constructive dismissal.

Constructive dismissal may occur if the employer breaks an express term of the contract, such as by reducing pay (*Industrial Rubber Products v Gillon* [1977]) or failing to follow a prescribed disciplinary procedure (*Post Office v Strange* [1981]). It can also occur if there is a breach of an implied term, such as the duty to provide a reasonably suitable working environment (*Waltons and Morse v Dorrington* [1977]), the duty to provide access to a grievance procedure (*WA Goold (Pearmak) Ltd v McConnell and Another* [1995]) or the duty to maintain mutual trust and confidence. Some case illustrations of breaches of the latter term follow:

- failing to respond to an employee's complaints about the lack of adequate safety equipment (*British Aircraft Corp v Austin* [1978]);

- failing to provide an employee with reasonable support to enable him to carry out his job without disruption and harassment from fellow employees (*Wigan BC v Davies* [1979]);

- ▦ failing to properly investigate allegations of sexual harassment or to treat the complaint with sufficient seriousness (*Bracebridge Engineering Ltd v Darby* [1990]);

- ▦ imposing a disciplinary penalty grossly out of proportion to the offence (*BBC v Beckett* [1983]);

- ▦ a series of minor incidents of harassment over time which cumulatively amount to repudiation: the so called 'last straw doctrine' (*Woods v WM Car Services (Peterborough)* [1982]).

▶ BBC v BECKETT [1983]

Beckett was a scenic carpenter for the employer who was given notice of his dismissal for what the employer considered a 'serious breach of working practice'. This was due to him leaving his work in a dangerous condition with the resulting injury of a colleague.

Following an internal appeal, Beckett was offered an alternative job as a building maintenance carpenter. This was permitted under the terms of the contract, but the EAT held that the downgrading established a constructive dismissal. If the contract acts in a way which, when viewed objectively, amounts to a fundamental breach, then this can constitute a repudiation of the contract.

The implied duty of trust and confidence appears, at times, to override an employer's strict rights under the contract. In other words, employers must exercise their contractual powers in such a way as not to destroy trust and confidence: *United Bank Ltd v Akhtar* [1989]; *White v Reflecting Roadstuds Ltd* [1991]; *Bass Leisure Ltd v Thomas* [1994].

▶ UNITED BANK LTD v AKHTAR [1989]

Akhtar had been employed by the bank under a contract that contained a mobility clause which enabled the bank to require his transfer to any other part of the UK, on payment of a discretionary relocation allowance.

Approximately nine years following the commencement of his employment, Akhtar was given six days' notice to transfer from Leeds to Birmingham. Akhtar requested additional time for the move, and annual leave, but these requests went unanswered. Akhtar claimed he had been constructively dismissed and the EAT agreed. There was an implied term that the mobility clause would be invoked reasonably, and the actions of the bank were sufficient to fundamentally breach the trust and confidence between the parties.

A constructive dismissal is not necessarily unfair: *Savoia v Chiltern Herb Farms Ltd* [1982].

An employee, who is in material breach of the implied term of trust and confidence at the time of the resignation, is not entitled to end the contract of employment and claim constructive dismissal. (See the EAT's reasoning in *Aberdeen City Council v McNeill* [2009] where Lady Smith stated 'If a party to such a contract is in material breach of one of his obligations he cannot insist that the other party perform a reciprocal term.')

As constructive dismissals involve an employee resigning from the employment, it is necessary for the tribunal to identify the 'final straw' that led to the resignation. This will enable a determination as to whether the claimant was entitled to resign or not (*Wishaw and District Housing Association Limited v Moncrieff* [2009]).

Following a claim of constructive dismissal, the tribunal is to follow the Court of Appeal's decision in *Buckland v Bournemouth University Higher Education Corporation* [2010]. The test as to whether the employer has fundamentally breached the contract is a unitary test and should not follow a 'range of reasonable responses' test. The decision is also important as it provides authority that having fundamentally breached the contract, the employer cannot later 'fix it' by some action while the employee contemplates whether or not to treat the employer's action as a dismissal.

FACTS DISCOVERED AFTER THE DISMISSAL

In contrast to unfair dismissal protection, a summary dismissal that would have constituted a wrongful dismissal can be justified at the hearing through the submission of evidence that proves the employer was correct in dismissing.

> ▶ BOSTON DEEP SEA FISHING AND ICE CO v ANSELL [1888]
>
> The employee was the managing director of a company who was accused of dishonesty and was, as a consequence, summarily dismissed by the employer. At the time of the dismissal the employer had no tangible evidence, but later discovered that the employee had been taking bribes in awarding contracts. This act was a fundamental breach of the duty of good faith and the evidence established the employer's action as justified.

ENFORCEMENT PROCEEDINGS

Wrongful dismissals generally consist of those terminations of the employment contract where the correct notice period has not been provided and which cannot be justified by the employer.

The claimant in a wrongful dismissal claim may seek damages as the primary method of compensation, and this is limited to the notice period – either reasonable, contractual or statutory-based.

Wrongful dismissal may be advantageous where the worker does not qualify for protection under unfair dismissal legislation, his/her claim is more valuable than the maximum available under statute, or where the time period for a claim under unfair dismissal has expired.

Specific performance is not (generally) possible in contracts of personal service due to the requirement of constant supervision that is not practical in such contracts.

Injunctions are available (*Lumley v Wagner* [1852]) to stop an individual from breaching his/her contract (*Warner Bros v Nelson* [1937]). They have also been used to stop an employer from breaching a contractual disciplinary procedure (*Gryf-Lowczowski v Hinchingbrooke Healthcare NHS Trust* [2006]).

You should now be confident that you would be able to tick all the boxes on the checklist at the beginning of this chapter. To check your knowledge of Termination of employment why not visit the companion website and take the Multiple Choice Question test. Check your understanding of the terms and vocabulary used in this chapter with the flashcard glossary.

5

Unfair dismissal

Protection under unfair dismissal is only available to employees who qualify as being continuously employed by the employer for at least one year; have been (unfairly) dismissed; and have submitted a claim within three months of the dismissal

Some dismissals are automatically unfair – those to do with the individual's pregnancy; trade union membership/activities etc – these do not require the one year's continuous service

Section 98 Employment Rights Act (ERA) 1996 identifies potentially fair reasons for the employer to dismiss the employee

Reasons discovered after the dismissal will not justify an unfair dismissal but may reduce any compensation awarded

An employer's action to dismiss will be judged against a 'band of reasonable responses' test – the tribunal must not substitute its own view of whether it would have dismissed in the circumstances

The employer does not need proof of an employee's misconduct to (potentially) justify a dismissal, only objective and reasonable grounds for holding the belief.

The remedies for unfair dismissal include compensation, re-engagement, or reinstatement

Employees have the (conditional) right not to be unfairly dismissed (ERA s 94).

UNFAIR DISMISSAL

Unfair dismissal	● Time limit in which to lodge a claim is usually three months
	● Remedies – compensation, reinstatement or re-engagement
	● Limit on compensation
	● Forum – employment tribunal (Employment Appeal Tribunal on appeal)
	● Proceedings – relatively informal
	● Employee must have been employed for qualifying period – currently one year – for the majority of dismissals
	● Compensation can be reduced by up to 25 per cent for failure to follow ACAS Code of Practice
	● Acts or omissions discovered after dismissal are not relevant to the fairness issue (though they could reduce compensation)
Wrongful dismissal	● Under the Limitation Act 1980, the time limit for claims is six years
	● Compensation is only awarded on the basis of Addis [1909]
	● No limit on compensation
	● Forum – county court or High Court (appeal to the Court of Appeal or, in Scotland, to the Court of Session). Since 1994, employment tribunals have had the jurisdiction to hear termination of contract claims of up to £25,000, with some exceptions, such as covenants in restraint of trade
	● Usual court rules and formalities apply
	● No qualifying period
	● No age limit
	● No account is taken of the employee's action contributing to dismissal
	● Acts or omissions discovered after dismissal will be taken into account in determining fairness

STAGE 1: HAS A DISMISSAL TAKEN PLACE?

THE MEANING OF DISMISSAL

This was discussed in Chapter 4. The term covers express dismissal, the expiry of a fixed term contract and constructive dismissal.

STAGE 2: IS THE APPLICANT QUALIFIED TO MAKE A CLAIM?

The following are necessary components to qualify:

■ The individual has 'employee' status.

- He/she has been continuously employed for at least one year.

- He/she has been dismissed (and unfairly).

- He/she has submitted the claim within three months of the effective date of termination.

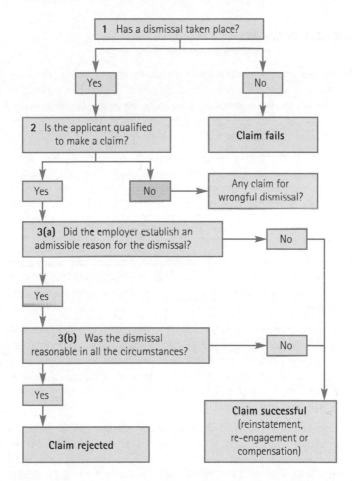

There are three issues here:

- Is the applicant an 'employee'? (See Chapter 1)
- Does the applicant's employment fall within an excluded category?
- Has the applicant presented the claim in time?

EXCLUDED CATEGORIES

Excluded categories include the following:

- Workers engaged in official action who, at the time of their dismissal, are taking industrial action or are locked out where there has been no selective dismissal or re-engagement of those taking the action. Unofficial strikers may be selectively dismissed or re-engaged (ss 237 and 238 of the Trade Union and Labour Relations (Consolidation) Act (TULR(C)A) 1992).

- Individuals taking part in industrial action who are sacked within eight weeks of the start of the action are deemed to be unfairly dismissed. Protection extends beyond the eight-week period if the employers have not taken reasonable steps to resolve the dispute (Employment Relations Act 1999).

- Illegal contracts: a contract of employment to do an unlawful act is unenforceable.

- Those employees covered by a disciplinary procedure, voluntarily agreed between employers and an independent trade union, where the Secretary of State has designated it to apply instead of the statutory scheme (s 110 of the ERA 1996).

- Where a settlement of the claim has been agreed with the involvement of an ACAS conciliation officer and the employee has agreed to withdraw his/her complaint (s 203(2)(e) of the ERA 1996), and where the employee enters into a valid compromise contract satisfying the conditions set out in s 203(3). These include the condition that the employee should have taken independent legal advice.

In most cases, continuous employment for one calendar year is required in order to claim unfair dismissal. It is therefore necessary to identify the effective date of termination (see below). A statutory definition of continuous employment is given in ss 210–13 of the ERA (see also *Ford v Warwickshire County Council* [1983]; *Flack v Kodak Ltd* [1987]; cf *Booth v USA* [1999]).

Strikes do not break continuity of employment but time on strike is not counted towards the one-year qualifying period.

CLAIM IN TIME

In common with the enforcement of most other employment protection rights, an applicant must present a claim within three months of the effective date of termination. This time limit is fairly rigorously applied, although it confers upon employment tribunals a discretion to allow a claim to be presented within a reasonable time outside the three-month period where it considers that it was not reasonably practicable for the complaint to be presented in time (s 111 of the ERA 1996).

The leading cases in this area state that the test to be applied in determining whether a late claim should be considered is not confined to whether the applicant knew of the right to claim, but extends to a consideration of whether he *should* have known: *Dedman v British Building and Engineering Appliances* [1974]; *Walls Meat Co Ltd v Khan* [1987]. Illness is an example of a valid reason for delay. Erroneous advice as to the time limits given to the applicant by a 'skilled adviser', such as a lawyer, trade union official or Citizens Advice Bureau worker, will not excuse a late application: *Riley v Tesco Stores Ltd* [1980] – any claim for negligent misstatement lies against the adviser. However, where the erroneous advice was given by an employment tribunal clerk, this does provide an excuse for a late claim: *Jean Sorelle Ltd v Rybak* [1991]. It is a question of fact – as opposed to a question of law – whether it was 'reasonably practicable' to claim in time: *Palmer v Southend on Sea BC* [1984].

> ### ▶ MILLER v COMMUNITY LINKS TRUST LTD [2007]
>
> Here the claimant was assisted in the claim by a second-year law student (who incidentally was charging £120 per hour for their services).
>
> The ET 1 claim was submitted electronically one second before midnight of the three-month deadline but this did not reach the Employment Tribunal Service until eight seconds after the deadline had passed.
>
> Here the Employment Appeal Tribunal (EAT) confirmed that the claim was out of time.

The case demonstrated that even though only 9 seconds out of time, this was still a claim out of time and hence, if the tribunal considered that it was reasonably practicable to submit on time, it was not in a position to consider the facts. This judgment follows *Marks and Spencer Plc v William Ryan* [2005] where the case involved electronic submission that was 88 seconds out of time, which, again, was time-barred from being heard.

Miller is also relevant as the Compensation Act 2006 (s 4(1)) in force since 23 April 2007, prohibits non-legally qualified advisors from representing a litigant unless this is for free or in other very limited circumstances, unless they are registered with the regulating body (the Regulated Claims Management Service).

In *John Lewis Partnership v Charman* [2011] the EAT held that if an employee is reasonably ignorant of the applicable time limits of lodging an unfair dismissal claim before he/she has received the outcome of an internal appeal procedure against dismissal, but then does submit within a reasonable period thereafter, the claim will not necessarily be time-barred. The tribunal has the discretion to determine what 'reasonably practicable' means in relation to the facts of a case.

THE EFFECTIVE DATE OF TERMINATION (s 97)

The qualifying period is calculated up to and including the effective date of termination. The ERA 1996 offers a statutory definition of the date of termination for both unfair dismissal and redundancy payment claims and, although it is called the 'effective date of termination' for unfair dismissal purposes and the 'relevant date' for redundancy payments, the definition is largely the same in both situations. The effective date of termination (EDT) is defined as follows:

▪ Where the contract of employment is terminated by notice, whether by employer or employee, the date of termination is the date on which the notice expires (ss 97(1)(a) and 145(2)(a)). Whether provided in oral or written form (unless otherwise provided for in the contract), contractual notice runs from the day after the notice is given (*Wang v University of Keele* [2010]).

▪ Where the contract of employment is terminated without notice, the date of termination is the date on which the termination takes effect (ss 97(1)(b) and 145(1)(b)). If an employee is summarily dismissed with wages in lieu of notice, the 'effective date of termination' is the actual date on which the employee is told of dismissal, and not the date on which the appropriate notice period would expire (*Robert Cort & Sons v Charman* [1981]; *Stapp v Shaftesbury Society* [1982]; *Batchelor v BRB* [1987]).

▨ Where the employee is employed under a contract for a fixed/limited term, the date of termination is the date on which the term expires.

The EDT is to be judged objectively from the facts and it is not available to the parties to determine this between themselves (*Fitzgerald v University of Kent at Canterbury* [2004]). The Supreme Court held in *Gisada Syf v Barratt* [2010] that the EDT when an employee was sent a letter of dismissal by recorded post, and she did not read it as she was not expecting the letter, was when she returned home and opened (and read) its contents. The employee had not deliberately failed to read it, nor had she gone away from home for a few days with the intention of avoiding the letter. The Supreme Court remarked that it was desirable to interpret s 97 in a way favourable to the employee.

STAGE 3: IS THE DISMISSAL FAIR OR UNFAIR?

See s 98(4) of the ERA 1996.

REASON FOR THE DISMISSAL: POTENTIALLY FAIR REASONS

It is required that the employer demonstrates the (potentially fair) reason for the employee's dismissal. However, also note that where an employee disputes the reason given by the employer (for example, whistleblowing) the burden does not switch to the employee but rather the employer simply has to produce some evidence in support of that assertion (*Kuzel v Roche* [2008]). Here, Mummery L J stated that the employer had dismissed the employee for a reason – the employer knew what it was and must prove what it was.

See s 98(1)–(2) of the ERA 1996.

▨ Capability or qualifications (s 98(2)(a)), examples include developing illnesses and being incapable to perform the job (but the employee must have been trained or professed to have the capability).

> ▶ DAVISON v KENT METERS [1975]

A woman was employed at an assembly plant and was dismissed when it was discovered she had assembled over 470 (of 500 units) incorrectly.

She claimed it was due to the way the chargehand had instructed her, although the chargehand denied this.

The tribunal decided that either the company had not given her correct training, or this was the way she had been instructed to assemble the units, so the dismissal was unfair.

▪ Conduct (s 98(2)(b)), such as disobedience and theft.

> ▶ PEPPER v WEBB [1969]

An employee was employed as a gardener, whose work and attitude had recently diminished, and when asked to undertake some planting he responded 'I couldn't care less about your bloody greenhouse and your sodding garden.' He was summarily dismissed.

The Court of Appeal held that the employee's wilful disobedience of the employer's lawful order amounted to a fundamental breach of the contract and justified the summary dismissal.

But note that warnings should be used where the act of the employee does not constitute a 'gross' misconduct (ACAS Code of Practice on Disciplinary and Grievance Procedures). Expired warnings should not be used when contemplating action (*Airbus UK v Webb* [2007]) and Elias P in the decision quoted the case of *Diosynth v Thomson* [2006] that 'a tribunal is obliged, and not merely entitled, to ignore expired warnings'.

> ▶ MONIE v CORAL RACING [1981]

The claimant worked as an area manager of 19 betting shops. Only he and his assistant had access to the company's safe and whilst he was on annual leave his assistant discovered there was a substantial sum of money missing.

During an investigation there was no evidence of a break-in or that the safe had been forcibly opened, and, as neither the manager nor his assistant accepted responsibility, the EAT held that both could be dismissed for misconduct.

An employer should also be forthright in any allegations he/she puts to an employee. In *Celebi v Scolarest Compass Group UK & Ireland Ltd* [2010] the EAT held that an internal disciplinary hearing's finding of an employee's guilt of theft of £3,000 was unfair. The employer had worded the allegation put to her as 'loss of £3,000' rather than 'theft of £3,000' and under the (repealed) statutory disciplinary procedures (the Employment Act 2002 (Dispute Resolution) Regulations 2004), the required Step 1 letter did not accurately set out the charge against the employee.

The Court of Appeal provided an important judgment in *Salford Royal NHS Foundation Trust v Roldan* [2010]. The more serious the consequences for an employee following a dismissal, the greater the care that must be exercised in any investigation. In this case, the employee faced being deported as a result of a dismissal.

▪ Redundancy (s 98(2)(c)) (see Chapter 6 for the definition) (this includes unfair selection).

▪ The employee cannot continue to work without contravention of a statute (s 98(2)(d)), (for example when a delivery driver loses his/her driving licence).

> ▶ **FOUR SEASONS HEALTHCARE LTD v MAUGHAN [2005]**
>
> A registered nurse was convicted of offences against patients and therefore he was unable to work with them.
>
> As such, the contract was held to be frustrated, but would have enabled the employer to dismiss the employee from the care home in which he had been employed.

■ Some other substantial reason (SOSR) (s 98(1)(b)), such as when a customer exerts pressure on the employer to dismiss the employee or an employee refuses to accept new contractual terms of employment.

▶ RS COMPONENTS v IRWIN [1973]

An employer was subject to previous employees starting up new businesses in the same area and 'poaching' his employees (who had knowledge of his business) and this was affecting the profitability of the firm.

As a consequence, he required all his current employees to sign restraint of trade clauses to prevent them working for competitors for a given time following leaving the employment. One who refused was dismissed and it was held to be fair due to SOSR.

It is important to note that the requirement of the reasons for the dismissal is not proof of the reason, but merely that the employer had honest and reasonable grounds to hold the belief, and that this was the principal reason for the dismissal (*BHS v Burchell* [1978]).

Where a dismissal has been due to the employee's conduct which has caused a breakdown in the trust and confidence between the parties, such a dismissal will be SOSR and therefore, as it is not for 'conduct', the employer does not have to follow its own conduct dismissal procedures (*Ezsias v North Glamorgan NHS Trust* [2011]).

(REPEAL OF) THE DEFAULT RETIREMENT AGE

On the 13th January 2011, the Department for Business, Innovation & Skills (DBIS) confirmed the abolition of the default retirement age (of 65 years) from 1st October 2011. The Employment Equality (Repeal of Retirement Age Provisions) Regulations 2011 is the law that abolished the retirement age, reg 4 of which revokes schedule 6 of the Employment Equality (Age) Regulations 2006 (duty of the employer to consider an employee's request to work beyond retirement). Hence, where reg 5(1) was complied with, an employee could be retired for the purposes of his/her age (this was, until commencement of this legislation, a sixth potentially fair reason to dismiss). After this date, the use of a default retirement age would not be a potentially fair reason to dismiss a worker under s 98 ERA 1996.

Due to the obvious concerns employers had about an aging workforce and potentially being in breach of the law where they attempted to dismiss an employee due to age, a phasing in period was introduced. The phasing in of the provisions began in April 2011 to enable employers to make the necessary adjustments to their policies and procedures. This led to much concern over the implementation of the abolition as employers had until the 5th April 2011 to provide affected employees with (the maximum) 12-months' notice of intention to be retired, and to whom they granted a six-month extension (thereby not have to give the employee fresh notice of the intention to retire and consequent problems this may bring). Hence, 5th October 2012 will be the date DBIS identifies as the last date for retirement under the old law.

The law is contained in The Employment Equality (Repeal of Retirement Age Provisions) Regulations 2011 which provides:

- Employees can be lawfully retired provided the notice of the intention to retire was given by the 5th April 2011 AND the employee had attained the age of 65 by 30th September 2011 (reg 5(1)).

- The 5th January 2012 is the last date an employee may exercise a right to request to work beyond retirement (reg 5(4)).

Employers were concerned about the effect the Regulations might have for their business (not being able to dismiss workers having reached the retirement age). However, in *Seldon v Clarkson, Wright & Jakes (A Partnership) & Anor* [2010], the Court of Appeal held that a compulsory retirement age of 65 could be justified (here in relation to partners of a law firm). The Court found that the EU Framework Directive allowed Member States to derogate from direct age discrimination (which the UK did through reg 3 of the Employment Equality (Age) Regulations 2006) where the treatment is a proportionate means of achieving a legitimate aim. Hence, both direct and indirect forms of discrimination in this context may be justified by an employer. Further, the aims of the State in this respect – legitimate social policy objectives – as noted in *The Incorporated Trustees of the National Council on Ageing (Heyday) v BERR* [2009], were not applicable to private employers. Instead, employers have discretion/flexibility as to what a legitimate aim may be. Surely, case law will provide scope for argument and analysis of this point of law.

REASONS DISCOVERED AFTER DISMISSAL

An employer will only be allowed to rely upon facts known at the time of the dismissal to establish what was the reason for the dismissal. Facts that come to light after the dismissal cannot be relied upon to justify the dismissal, though they may persuade a tribunal to reduce compensation: *W Devis & Sons Ltd v Atkins* [1977].

However, evidence of actions that would breach the fundamental terms of a contract of employment and hence enable a fair dismissal have to be presented in time to the original tribunal.

▶ HYGIA PROFESSIONAL TRAINING v CUTTER [2007]

Here the employer did not bring evidence to the tribunal to prove the employee had been attempting to poach customers as he did not know he was supposed to present this information.

On appeal against the tribunal's decision, the EAT held that whilst the employer was now able to produce four witnesses (and over-whelming evidence) to substantiate his allegations, there was no credible reason why this could not have been presented in the first case, and ignorance or poor advice does not create a justification for new evidence as a ground for appeal.

DISMISSALS WHICH ARE DEEMED TO BE UNFAIR

Certain reasons for dismissal are regarded as automatically unfair and do not require one years' continuous employment before claims may be made. These are as follows:

- Dismissal for trade union membership and activity, where the union is independent, or for a refusal to join a trade union or particular trade union, whether the union is independent or not (s 152 of TULR(C)A 1992).

- Dismissal for taking part in industrial action within eight weeks of the start of the strike or within a longer period if the employers do not take reasonable steps to resolve the dispute (Employment Relations Act 1999).

- Dismissal of a woman because she is pregnant, for a reason connected with her pregnancy or childbirth or for making use of maternity laws (s 99 of the ERA 1996).

▨ Dismissal because of a conviction which is spent under the terms of the Rehabilitation of Offenders Act 1974 (s 4(3)(b)).

▨ Dismissal connected with the transfer of an undertaking, unless there are economic, technical or organisational reasons entailing changes in the workforce (see reg 7(3) of the Transfer of Undertakings (Protection of Employment) Regulations 2006).

▨ Dismissal on the ground of redundancy if the circumstances constituting the redundancy also applied equally to one or more employees in the same undertaking who held posts similar to that held by the dismissed employee and who have not been dismissed and:

- ● the reason (or, if more than one, the principal reason) for selecting the employee for dismissal was union related (s 153 of TULR(C)A 1992); or
- ● the reason for selection was because of pregnancy or childbirth or because the employee had: been involved in raising or taking action on health and safety issues; asserted certain statutory rights (see below); performed (or proposed to perform) any functions as a trustee of an occupational pension scheme; performed (or proposed to perform) the functions or activities of an employee representative for the purpose of consultation over redundancies or the transfer of an undertaking or as a 'protected' or 'opted out' shop or betting worker; or refused to work on a Sunday.

▨ Dismissal on the grounds that the employee

- ● carried out, or proposed to carry out, duties as a safety representative or as a member of a safety committee;
- ● where there was no representative or committee, or it was not reasonable to raise the matter with them, brought to the employer's attention, by reasonable means, harmful or potentially harmful circumstances;
- ● left the place of work, or refused to return to it, in circumstances of danger which the employee reasonably believed to be serious or imminent and which he could not reasonably have been expected to avert; or
- ● in circumstances of danger, took or proposed to take appropriate steps to protect himself or others from the danger (s 100 of the ERA 1996).

▨ Dismissal where the employee brought proceedings against the employer to enforce a 'relevant statutory right' or alleged an infringement of such a right. 'Relevant statutory rights' are those conferred by the ERA 1996, for which the remedy is by way of complaint to an employment tribunal; notice rights under s 86 of the ERA; and rights relating to deductions from pay, union activities and time off under TULR(C)A 1992.

▨ Dismissal of an employee who is a trustee of an occupational pension scheme established under a trust if the reason (or, if more than one, the principal reason) for the dismissal is that the employee performed (or proposed to perform) any of the functions of a trustee (s 102 of the ERA 1996).

▨ Dismissal of a 'protected' or 'opted out' shop or betting worker for refusing to work on a Sunday or for giving (or proposing to give) an opting out notice to the employer (s 101 of the ERA 1996). Broadly, shop or betting workers are 'protected' if, before the commencement dates of the legislation which liberalised Sunday trading and betting, they were not required under their contract of employment to work on Sunday. Shop or betting workers who are contractually required to work on Sunday may give three months' written notice of their intention to 'opt out' of Sunday working at the end of the notice period, but not before (Pt IV of the ERA 1996).

▨ Dismissal for making a protected public interest disclosure (s 103A of the ERA 1996); for the meaning of 'protected disclosure', see Pt IVA of the ERA 1996: both of these provisions were inserted by the Public Interest Disclosure Act 1998.

THE REASONABLENESS OF THE DISMISSAL

If the dismissal is not deemed to be unfair ('automatically unfair'), the tribunal considers its fairness. See s 98(4) of ERA 1996:

> ... the determination of the question whether the dismissal is fair or unfair (having regard to the reason shown by the employer):
> (a) depends on whether, in the circumstances (including the size and administrative resources of the employer's undertaking), the employer acted reasonably or unreasonably in treating it as a sufficient reason for dismissing the employee; and
> (b) shall be determined in accordance with equity and the substantial merits of the case.

In *Iceland Frozen Foods v Jones* [1983], the EAT summed up the correct approach for the tribunal to adopt in answering the question posed by s 98(4) as follows:

- the starting point should always be the words of s 98(4);

- in applying the section, the tribunal must consider the reasonableness of the employer's conduct, not simply whether they (the members of the tribunal) consider the dismissal to be fair;

- in judging the reasonableness of the employer's conduct, a tribunal must not substitute its own decision as to what was the right course to adopt for that of the employer;

- in many (though not all) cases, there is a band of reasonable responses to the employee's conduct, within which one employer might reasonably take one view and another may quite reasonably take another;

- the function of the tribunal, as an industrial jury, is to determine whether, in the particular circumstances of each case, the decision to dismiss fell within the band of reasonable responses which a reasonable employer might have adopted. If the dismissal falls within the band, the dismissal is fair; if it falls outside the band, it is unfair.

PROCEDURAL FAIRNESS

By the late 1970s, there had been a dilution of procedural requirements. The high point in this trend was to be found in the test laid down by the EAT in *British Labour Pump Co Ltd v Byrne* [1979]. This test allowed the employer to argue that an element of procedural unfairness (such as a failure to give a proper hearing) could be 'forgiven' if the employer could show that, on the balance of probabilities, even if a proper procedure had been complied with, the employee would still have been dismissed and the dismissal would still have been fair.

This test was overruled by the House of Lords in *Polkey v AE Dayton Services* [1987]. In the speeches, there is a re-emphasis of the importance of following a fair procedure. In the view of Lord Bridge of Harwich:

> ... an employer having *prima facie* grounds to dismiss ... will, in the great majority of cases, not act reasonably in treating the reason

as a sufficient reason for dismissal unless and until he has taken the steps, conveniently classified in most of the authorities as 'procedural', which are necessary in the circumstances of the case to justify that course of action.

Lord Mackay of Clashfern was of the opinion that what must be considered is what a reasonable employer would have had in mind at the time he decided to dismiss the employee(s):

If the employer could reasonably have concluded, in the light of the circumstances known to him at the time of the dismissal, that consultation or warning would be useless, he might well act reasonably even if he did not observe the provisions of the code.

The *Polkey* decision should also be viewed alongside the earlier House of Lords ruling in *West Midlands Co-operative Society Ltd v Tipton* [1986]. As with *Polkey*, the point at issue was the precise scope of the *Devis v Atkins* principle. Ever since *Devis v Atkins* [1977], it was not clear whether and to what extent that decision prevented matters arising out of internal appeals from being considered by employment tribunals as part of their assessment of 'reasonableness'. In *Tipton*, the Lords confirmed that both the denial of a contractual right of appeal and matters arising out of an appeal, if one is held, can be taken into account by tribunals when they assess the reasonableness of the employer's conduct.

ACAS CODE OF PRACTICE AND PROCEDURAL FAIRNESS

Following enactment of the Employment Act 2008, the previous statutory dispute resolution procedures were repealed. This allowed for greater flexibility in grievance, disciplinary and dismissal procedures in resolving workplace disputes (involving repeal of the mandatory three-stage procedure). ACAS has produced a 'Code of Practice 1 – Disciplinary and Grievance Procedures' identifying how the employer and employee should conduct themselves during grievance/disciplinary matters, and the tribunal will consider whether the parties followed the code in determining the reasonableness of any action taken in such proceedings. The tribunal is empowered to adjust any award by up to 25% for an unreasonable failure to follow the code. The code is not law, but it is referred to by tribunals when assessing the reasonableness of an employer's decision to dismiss.

Features to be considered by the parties in the event of disciplinary/grievance matters include:

- The parties should raise issues quickly and these should be dealt with in a prompt manner – with no unreasonable delays.

- The employer should carry out a reasonable investigation to ascertain the facts.

- The employer should present his/her concerns to the employee and give him/her an opportunity to respond before a decision is made.

- The employer should follow the Employment Relations Act 1999 ss 10–13 regarding the right of the worker to be accompanied at formal disciplinary/ grievance meetings by a colleague/trades union official.

- An appeal against the decision of the employer should be offered to the affected employee.

Right to be accompanied

The worker (a broader definition than 'employee') has a right to be accompanied to a disciplinary and grievance hearing by a work colleague or a trade union official (Employment Relations Act 1999 ss 10–13). In *Bullock v Norfolk County Council* [2010] the EAT held a foster carer is not a worker for the purposes of ERA 1996 or the Employment Relations Act 1999. Hence, such an individual has no right be accompanied at a meeting.

The Court of Appeal has stated in *Kulkarni v Milton Keynes Hospital NHS Trust* [2009] that NHS doctors are entitled to legal representation (not just a work colleague or trade union official) when faced with charges of misconduct/ capability under the terms of their contracts (and albeit *obiter*, that legal representation should be extended to anyone who may be unable to work in the future following successful charges against them (based on Art. 6 of European Convention on Human Rights right to a fair trial)). A similar ruling was provided earlier by the High Court in *R (on the application of G) v The Governors of X School* [2009] regarding a music assistant at X school. Further, the High Court has ruled that Art. 6 is not engaged in internal disciplinary procedures if the effect is not to deprive an employee of a right to practice his/her profession (*Puri, R (on the application of) v Bradford Teaching Hospitals NHS Foundation Trust* [2011]).

APPEALS

An appeal from a tribunal will be heard at the EAT. In *Fuller v London Borough of Brent* [2011] the Court of Appeal provided some useful guidance on the principles of appeals in a case relating to the EAT's decision to overturn a finding of unfair dismissal in a misconduct case. Some of the more important are:

- The appeal body being mindful not to substitute its own response to the employee's conduct for that formed by the tribunal. This in turn requires that the appellate body distinguish between a genuine question of law and a question of fact 'disguised' as a question of law.
- It should not be overly 'fussy' regarding the judgment nor be hypercritical of the style adopted.
- The tribunal should provide specific answers to legal questions asked (e.g. regarding the reasonableness of investigations). This detail will hopefully dissuade unnecessary or optimistic appeals. (This final point was a comment of general application.)

STAGE 4: REMEDIES

Remedies include:

- an order for reinstatement (s 114);
- an order for re-engagement (s 115);
- an award of compensation (s 118).

'Reinstatement' means putting the employee back into his/her own job as if the dismissal had never taken place. This is the principal remedy following an unfair dismissal. 'Re-engagement' is defined as putting the applicant into a similar job (hence they are orders for redeployment). Rights (such as the use of a company car) lost between dismissal and redeployment may be the subject of financial orders.

Reinstatement orders are subject to the requirements of s 116 of the ERA 1996, but the EAT has also held that mutual trust and confidence must also be present (and have not been destroyed) or redeployment must not be ordered (*Central & NW London NHS Trust v Abimbola* [2009]).

COMPENSATION

The rules relating to the calculation of unfair dismissal compensation can be summarised as follows.

The basic award (s 119 of the ERA 1996)

An award of half, one, or one and a half weeks' pay for each year of continuous service (depending on age), subject to a maximum of 20 years. A week's pay is calculated in accordance with ss 220–29 of the ERA 1996, and is based on gross pay (to a maximum of £400). As of 1st February 2011, the maximum award is £12,000 (i.e. 30 × £400).

The term 'week's pay' is subject to a statutory maximum, which is amended each year.

Basic award and age

If aged	But less than	No of weeks' pay for each year
	22	½
22	41	1
41	65	1½

Compensatory award

The tribunal may also make a compensatory award (s 123 of the ERA 1996). This is an amount which the tribunal considers 'just and equitable'. Both the basic and compensatory award may be reduced if the applicant contributed to his/her own dismissal or as a result of any conduct before dismissal. The maximum award under this head is subject to review on an annual basis. As of 1st February 2011, the maximum award is £68,400. Therefore the total award is up to a maximum of £80,400 (£68,400 compensatory award plus £12,000 basic award).

The aim of the award is to reimburse the employee for any financial loss experienced: interim loss of net earnings between the date of the dismissal and the tribunal hearing, and future losses that he is likely to sustain, including wages, pensions and other fringe benefits. The amount must be 'just and equitable', but will not include non-economic losses, such as injury to feelings. Sums are then deducted for, for example, contributory fault and failure to mitigate. The amount awarded by the tribunal is not affected by an employer's claim of an inability to pay. In *Tao Herbs & Acupuncture Ltd v Jin* [2010] the EAT held that such claims are not a relevant consideration under s 123.

The additional award

This award is made where an order for reinstatement or re-engagement is not complied with. The award is between 26 and 52 weeks' pay based on the maximum week's pay. As of 1st February 2011, the maximum award is £20,800 (52 × 400).

You should now be confident that you would be able to tick all the boxes on the checklist at the beginning of this chapter. To check your knowledge of Unfair dismissal why not visit the companion website and take the Multiple Choice Question test. Check your understanding of the terms and vocabulary used in this chapter with the flashcard glossary.

6

Redundancy payments

Redundancy payments are calculated in the same way as the basic award in unfair dismissal claims (albeit work under the age of 18 does not count towards the calculation)

The employee must qualify for protection as identified under the Employment Rights Act 1996

In a redundancy claim, there is a presumption of redundancy in the dismissal and the burden is placed on the employer to disprove this

There exist several situations where the employee leaving the employment will not constitute a dismissal which subsequently prohibits a claim for redundancy

Redundancy occurs when the business the employee worked at closes or where the employee becomes surplus to the requirements of the business

Workers' rights are protected through the Transfer of Undertakings (Protection of Employment) Regulations 2006 in the event of a business being sold

The employer is allowed to claim that post-transfer dismissals are due to an economic, technical or organisational reason, that can justify the employer's action

Employers have a duty to consult with the workforce or their representatives in the event of redundancies or transfers

THE STATUTORY PROTECTION IN CASES OF REDUNDANCY

See Pt XI of the Employment Rights Act (ERA) 1996 (ss 135–65). Payment is calculated in the same way as the basic award in unfair dismissal cases, except that years worked while under the age of 18 do not count.

PRE-CONDITIONS FOR PAYMENT

To qualify for redundancy payments, the following are necessary:

- the person made redundant was an 'employee';

- he/she was continuously employed for a period of two years, ending with the 'relevant date';

- he/she is not in one of the excluded categories;

- he/she was dismissed; and

- the dismissal was by reason of redundancy.

There is a presumption of redundancy (s 163(2)). Therefore, the burden of proof is on the employer to disprove redundancy.

SITUATIONS WHERE NO DISMISSAL IS DEEMED TO HAVE OCCURRED

The following are situations in which no dismissal is deemed to have occurred:

- suitable offer of renewal or re-engagement;

- offers of suitable employment by associated companies;

- where there is a 'relevant transfer' of an undertaking.

EMPLOYEES WHO LEAVE PREMATURELY

If an employee leaves employment, having been warned of the possibility of redundancy in the future, but before receiving notice of termination, there is no dismissal. This may have the effect of employees staying with the employer until redundancy is effective rather than proactively seeking alternative employment.

> ▶ MORTON SUNDOUR FABRICS LTD v SHAW [1966]

The employer informed the employee that the business would be closing down some time in the forthcoming year without providing an exact date. The employee found another job and left the employment and sought a redundancy payment.

It was held that he was not under notice of redundancy at the time of leaving and hence did not qualify for the payment.

DISMISSAL MUST BE BY REASON OF REDUNDANCY

Redundancy (broadly) covers two situations. The first is where the employer is closing the business, and the second involves the employee being surplus to the requirements of the employer.

In the first situation, the tribunal assesses if the operation of the business has ceased and if so, a redundancy situation has occurred. This is an objective test and the tribunal is not permitted to assess the necessity or business need for the cessation (*Moon v Homeworthy Furniture* [1977]).

'Redundancy' is defined in s 139 of the ERA 1996 as follows:

For the purposes of this Act, an employee who is dismissed shall be taken to be dismissed by reason of redundancy if the dismissal is attributable wholly or mainly to:

(a) the fact that his employer has ceased, or intends to cease:
   (i) to carry on the business for the purposes of which the employee was employed by him; or
   (ii) to carry on that business in the place where the employee was so employed; or

(b) the fact that the requirements of that business:
   (i) for employees to carry out work of a particular kind; or
   (ii) for employees to carry out work of a particular kind in the place where the employee was so employed by the employer, have ceased or diminished or are expected to cease or diminish.

Dismissals for misconduct, including being on strike, are not dismissals for redundancy.

111

DEFINITIONAL ANALYSIS OF WORK OF A PARTICULAR KIND

In analysis of the second example of redundancy, there is a redundancy situation where the amount of work remains the same but an event, such as a reorganisation, discloses that overstaffing exists. This is because the statutory definition requires a diminution in the number of employees to do work of a particular kind, as opposed to a diminution in the work itself: *McCrea v Cullen and Davison* [1988].

In *Safeway Stores plc v Burrell* [1997], Mr Burrell, a petrol station manager, was told that there would be a reorganisation of the management structure and that the post of 'petrol station manager' would disappear. It was to be replaced by a new post of 'petrol filling station controller' at a lower salary. Existing postholders could apply for the management posts, although, as there were fewer posts than managers, there would be redundancies. Mr Burrell declined the invitation to apply and brought a complaint of unfair dismissal. He argued that the new job was essentially the same as the old one, so there was no redundancy situation. The employer contended that it was a genuine redundancy, or, alternatively, that there was justification for the dismissal on the basis of 'some other substantial reason'. Mr Burrell's claim was upheld. Many of the jobs he had actually done (the 'functional' test) were still required, albeit by someone with a different job title. The employment tribunal chair looked at what Mr Burrell's contract required (the 'contract' test) and concluded that the job he was employed to do no longer existed.

The Employment Appeal Tribunal (EAT) allowed the appeal and remitted the case for reconsideration by another tribunal. It held that the correct test involved three stages:

- (a) Was the employee dismissed?

- (b) If so, had the requirements of the business for employees to carry out work of a particular kind 'ceased or diminished' (or were they expected to do so)?

- (c) If so, was the dismissal caused wholly or mainly by that state of affairs?

The key issue at stage (b), said the EAT, was whether there was a diminution in the business requirements for employees (note: 'employees' generally, not the employee specifically) and, in deciding that, tribunals should not introduce a 'contract' test whereby they just considered the specific tasks for which the applicant was employed. On this test see also *Shawkat v Nottingham City Hospital NHS Trust* [2001].

It is quite common that employees may be made redundant, and two or more roles are replaced by one wider role. In *Morgan v The Welsh Rugby Union* [2010] the EAT reiterated the principle that the guidance provided in *Williams v Compare Maxam* [1982] does not apply in redundancy situations where the employees are applying for a new and different role. Insofar as the process of selecting the applicant for the new role is conducted in a fair and objective manner, a dismissal of an employee who fails to be offered the (new, amalgamated) job will be fair.

BUMPING

'Bumping', or transferred redundancy, occurs when a person selected for redundancy is retained and another employee is dismissed in his/her place. In *Church v Lancashire NHS Trust* [1998], the EAT held that, as a matter of causation, the diminution or cessation in an employer's requirement for employees to carry out work of a particular kind must relate to the work carried out by the dismissed employee himself. Therefore, the EAT took the view that bumping does not fall within the statutory definition of redundancy.

However, the House of Lords, on appeal from the Northern Ireland case of *Murray v Foyle Meats Ltd* [1999], held that bumping was within the statutory definition of redundancy. Neither the 'contract' nor the 'functional' test was correct. One had to apply the pure words of the statute: has the employers' requirement for employees to do work of a particular kind ceased or diminished? If so, was the dismissal attributable to that? The fundamental question, following *Murray*, is whether the dismissal was wholly or mainly attributable to a redundancy situation – if so, the dismissal is by way of redundancy.

PLACE WHERE THE EMPLOYEE WAS EMPLOYED

The contractual approach has also been used to determine the 'place of employment'. This phrase has been interpreted to mean the place where the employee could be obliged to work under the terms of the contract of employment, not merely where the employee had been working prior to the instruction to move:

Sutcliffe v Hawker Siddeley Aviation [1973]; *UKAEA v Claydon* [1974]. This conventional approach was challenged in *Bass Leisure Ltd v Thomas* [1994], where the EAT ruled that the place where an employee was employed for redundancy payment purposes does not necessarily extend to any place where he could be contractually required to work, but is to be established by a factual inquiry, taking into account the employee's fixed or changing places of work and any contractual terms which evidence or define the place of employment and its extent, but not terms which provide for the employee to be transferred. The decision of the Court of Appeal in *High Table Ltd v Horst* [1997] approved the 'factual or geographical' test, as formulated in *Bass Leisure*, rather than the contractual test. These decisions will often make it easier to establish redundancy and allow the employer the best of both worlds with a mobility clause. If there is a mobility clause within the contract and the employee refuses to move, there may well be a fair dismissal. If, however, the employer does not choose to rely on the mobility clause when the work ceases or diminishes at the existing locality, the employer can still rely on redundancy in spite of the clause.

An employment contract cannot be silent on the place of work. If there is no express term, there must be an implied term. The geographical scope of the implied term depends on the circumstances of the case. Relevant factors include the nature of the employer's business; whether the employee has been moved during the course of the employment; what the employee was told when the employment started; and whether there are any provisions to cover expenses when working away from home: *O'Brien v Associated Fire Alarms Ltd* [1968]; *Stevenson v Teesside Bridge and Engineering Ltd* [1971]; *Jones v Associated Tunnelling Co Ltd* [1981]; *Courtaulds Northern Spinning Ltd v Sibson* [1988].

RE-ORGANISATION AND REDUNDANCY

There is no redundancy if the job function remains the same, even though there has been a substantial alteration in terms and conditions:

> ### ▶ NORTH RIDING GARAGES v BUTTERWICK [1967]
>
> The case involved a manager of a repairs workshop who had been employed at the garage for 30 years but had recently been moved

away from the more practical aspects of the job, to increasingly managerial aspects.

This involved more paperwork, which he did quite poorly, and was dismissed eight months following the movement to this new method of working due to incompetence. Butterwick's claim was that his dismissal was due to redundancy.

The court held that in fact the claimant had not been asked to perform a different type of work. Rather he was asked to adapt to new working methods, which he could be expected to do.

- *Vaux and Associated Brewers v Ward* [1970];
- *Chapman v Goonvean and Rostowrack China Clay* [1973];
- *Johnson v Nottinghamshire Combined Police Authority* [1974];
- *Lesney Products & Co Ltd v Nolan* [1977];
- cf *MacFisheries Ltd v Findlay* [1985].

The question to be asked, therefore, is whether the job itself has changed (= redundancy) or whether it is merely the way of doing the job which has changed (= question of adaptability).

RE-ORGANISATION AND UNFAIR DISMISSAL

As the cases listed above illustrate, where reorganisation causes a change in the employee's terms and conditions of employment, these changes may not fall within the legal concept of redundancy because the work that the employee does is not diminished. Can the imposition of such changes amount to unfair dismissal? The test of fairness is not inevitably controlled by the contract of employment. As a result, the courts and tribunals have been prepared to hold as fair dismissal cases where the employee has refused to agree to a change in terms and conditions in line with the employer's perception of business efficacy: see *Hollister v National Union of Farmers* [1979]; *St John of God (Care Services) Ltd v Brook* [1992].

UNREASONABLE REFUSAL OF SUITABLE ALTERNATIVE EMPLOYMENT

This will cause the employee to lose his right to a redundancy payment. The alternative must be objectively suitable. If so, whether the employee rejected it reasonably is assessed with regard to the particular employee. For example, the offer of a job in a 'floating pool' of teachers was not a suitable one for a head teacher because it reduced the status of the job: *Taylor v Kent CC* [1969]. In respect of the second issue (that is, whether the refusal is reasonable or not), a move from Mayfair to an office above a sex shop in Soho was unreasonably refused by a female employee: *Fuller v Stephanie Bowman Ltd* [1977].

Evidently, there may often be a balancing act to undertake between the suitability of an offer of alternative employment proposed by the employer, and the unreasonableness of a refusal to accept this by the employee. The EAT has held that a tribunal is entitled to have regard to the 'degree of suitability' of the alternative job offered by the employer in relation to the reasonableness or otherwise of a refusal by the employee to accept (*Commission for Healthcare Audit & Inspection v Ward* [2008]).

TRIAL PERIODS

An employee who wishes to try out an alternative job is given a trial period of four weeks by statute (s 138 of ERA 1996). If, however, he/she has been dismissed for redundancy, there is both a common law period of a reasonable length and the four-week statutory period.

UNFAIR REDUNDANCY DISMISSALS

Dismissal for redundancy may be attacked as unfair on three grounds:

- trade union/non-trade union membership or activity (s 153 of the Trade Union and Labour Relations (Consolidation) Act (TULR(C)A) 1992);

- the reason for the redundancy selection was because of pregnancy or childbirth or because the employee had made health and safety complaints or asserted certain statutory rights (s 105 of the ERA 1996);

- unreasonable redundancy under *Williams v Compair Maxam* [1982]. Here, the EAT set out five principles of good industrial relations practice that should generally be followed when employees are represented by a recognised trade union:

  (1) to give as much warning as possible;
  (2) to consult with the union, particularly relating to the criteria to be applied in selection for redundancy;

(3) to adopt objective rather than subjective criteria for selection, for example, experience, length of service, attendance, etc;

(4) to select in accordance with the criteria, considering any representations made by the union regarding selection;

(5) to consider the possibility of re-deployment rather than dismissal.

TRANSFER OF UNDERTAKINGS (PROTECTION OF EMPLOYMENT) REGULATIONS 2006

These complex regulations, as amended from time to time, seek to fulfil the UK's obligations under EC law to give effect to EC Council Directive 2001/23, generally known as the Acquired Rights Directive (ARD). The regulations provide that, where an undertaking is transferred from person A to person B:

▓ workers who are employed by A 'immediately before the transfer' automatically become the employees of B, retaining the same terms and conditions that they enjoyed with A;

▓ B assumes A's rights and liabilities in relation to those employees;

▓ any collective and union recognition agreements are transferred;

▓ A must inform recognised trade unions of the consequences of the transfer;

▓ dismissal of an employee (whether before or after transfer) for any reason connected with the transfer is automatically unfair unless the reason is for an 'economic, technical or organisational reason entailing changes in the workforce', in which case the dismissal is fair if reasonable in the circumstances.

The parties cannot contract out of the regulations.

RELEVANT TRANSFERS

None of the provisions in the regulations operates unless there is a 'relevant transfer' under reg 3(1), that is: 'a transfer of an economic entity which retains its identity' and reg 3(2) an economic entity is 'an organised grouping of resources which has the objective of pursuing an economic activity, whether or not that activity is central or ancillary'.

The Regulations are based on the ARD 2001, which in turn follows the case law established by the Court of Justice. In *Rygaard v Stro Molle* [1996] the Court of

Justice held that the undertaking must be a stable economic entity (and hence involving some level or permanence).

The Directive is wide enough to cover transfers of undertakings which are non-commercial in nature: see *Dr Sophie Redmond Stichting v Bartol* [1992], and this has been included in reg 3(4)(a) of TUPE 2006.

It is probable that a mere transfer of assets which falls short of a transfer of an undertaking as a going concern will fall outside the regulations. The Court of Justice has enunciated the test as to whether a stable economic entity has been transferred. In *Schmidt v Spar und Leihkasse der Früheren Amter Bordesholm, Kiel und Cronshagen* [1994], it held that there could be a transfer of contracted-out cleaning services, even where the services are performed by a single employee and there is no transfer of tangible assets. Contrast this approach to the Court of Justice's finding in *Suzen v Zehnacker Gebäudereingung GmbH Krankenhaus-service* [1997] that an activity does not, in itself, constitute a stable economic entity. Consequently, the Court of Justice stated, the mere fact that a similar activity is carried on before and after the change of contractors does not mean that there is a transfer of undertaking (see also *Betts v Brintel Helicopters Ltd and KLM ERA Helicopters (UK) Ltd* [1997]). Indeed, in relation to a change in service provider, this is where English and EU law differs. For the purposes of ARD 2001, a change of service provider is not a transfer of an undertaking (confirmed in *CLECE SA v Maria Socorro Martin Valor and Ayuntamiento de Cobisa* [2011]) whilst under TUPE 2006, change of a service provider IS a transfer of an undertaking.

The second form of transfer was added through TUPE 2006 reg 3, and provides for changes of service provider (including organisations such as firms of accountants, lawyers and so on). The Regulations widen the concept of relevant transfer which take the form of:

1 Contracting-out/out-sourcing (such as where a service previously undertaken by the client is awarded to a new contractor);
2 Re-tendering (such as where a contract for a service is awarded to a new contractor); and
3 Contracting-in/In-sourcing (such as where a contract with the previous contractor is performed 'in-house').

> ▶ HUNT v STORM COMMUNICATIONS, WILD CARD PUBLIC
> RELATIONS AND BROWN BROTHERS WINES [2008]
>
> Storm (a public relations consultancy firm) was employed to
> manage the public relations of Brown Brothers Wines (Europe).
> Hunt was employed by Storm as the account manger and spent
> approximately 70% of her working hours devoted to the Brown
> Brothers account. When the account was transferred to another
> firm, Hunt was designated an 'organised grouping of resources'
> under TUPE 2006 and as such the effect of the transfer of the
> service was that Hunt would transfer to the new firm taking over
> the account.

Note that the question of whether the contracting out of services constitutes a service provision for reg 3(1)(b) TUPE 2006 is a matter of law. However, the identification of the actual activities involved is a matter of fact (which an appeal court should not consider unless the decision of the tribunal is perverse). See *Ward Hadaway Solicitors v Capsticks Solicitors LLP* [2010].

EFFECT OF A TRANSFER ON CONTRACTS OF EMPLOYMENT

On a relevant transfer, the employee takes with him/her the contractual rights (reg 4), and claims against the transferor (such as sex discrimination – see *DJM International v Nicholas* [2006]) are transferred to the transferee (reg 10). It is arguable that personal injury claims are also transferred (*Bernudone v Pall Mall Services* [2000]).

It may be important to identify the precise time of the transfer because of the requirement that the employee is employed by the old employer immediately prior to the transfer. This was a big issue in earlier cases, but is less problematic following the decision of the House of Lords in *Litster v Forth Dry Dock and Engineering Co Ltd* [1989]. If the dismissal was connected to the transfer, then it will be caught by the regulations, irrespective of the precise timing of the dismissal (see also *P Bork International A/S v Forgeningen af Arbejdsledere i Danmark* [1989]).

> ▶ LITSTER v FORTH DRY DOCK AND ENGINEERING CO LTD
> [1989]
>
> Litster was one of twelve workers who had been continuously
> employed by the firm since 1981/1982 until the company became
> insolvent.
>
> On the day the company decided to cease trading a sale was
> arranged to another firm. One hour before the transfer was to take
> place the workforce was informed that the business was to close
> and consequently they were all dismissed with immediate effect.
>
> The House of Lords held that the workers had been employed by the
> transferor immediately before the transfer, and that their dismissal
> was connected to a transfer. Consequently the dismissals were
> subject to the Regulations and the former workers were entitled to
> compensation.

In *OTG Ltd v Barke* [2011] the EAT established that administration of an undertaking can never qualify as 'insolvency proceedings' for the purposes of reg 8(7)
TUPE 2006. As such, any employees employed immediately before the transfer
will have their contracts transferred under TUPE 2006.

Regulation 11 of TUPE 2006 requires the transferor to provide the transferee
with 'employee liability information' regarding the age of the employee, their
written particulars, and grievance procedure or disciplinary information.

ALTERING TERMS AND CONDITIONS

In the joined cases of *Wilson and Others v St Helens BC* [1998]; *Meade and
Baxendale v British Fuels Ltd* [1997], the crucial question is whether TUPE permits
changes in the terms and conditions to be agreed between the transferee and
employees whose work has been transferred. The Court of Justice held that such
an attempt was contrary to the ARD in *Daddy's Dance Hall* [1988]. The EAT held
that employees could not be bound by an agreement to vary their terms and
conditions if the transfer of the undertaking was the reason for the change. In
other words, employees could not be bound by a unilaterally imposed change, nor
would they be bound by a consensual change. Ultimately, this was the position

adopted by the House of Lords (see *Wilson v St Helens BC* [1998]; *Meade and Baxendale v British Fuels Ltd* [1998] (HL); see also *Credit Suisse First Boston (Europe) Ltd v Lister* [1998] (CA)).

> ### ▶ WILSON v ST HELENS BC [1998]
>
> Here the employees were made redundant by the transferor before the transfer, and then re-engaged by the transferee on poorer terms and conditions.
>
> They claimed their dismissals were void as they were in connection with the transfer. However, the House of Lords stated the dismissals were not void and hence their action should have been under unfair dismissal legislation (even though they were time-barred from accessing this right).

TUPE 2006 reg 4(4) provides that any attempted variation of employees' contracts will be held void if they are to do with a transfer that is not an economic, technical or organisational (ETO) reason.

Dismissal on a transfer of undertaking

Regulation 7 deems a dismissal caused by a transfer or for a reason connected with a transfer to be automatically unfair. It is not necessary for the transferor to have a specific transferee in mind when dismissing for reg 7 to be invoked (*Spaceright Europe Ltd v Baillavoine* [2011]). This position is modified by reg 7(3), which allows the employer to argue that the dismissal was for an 'economic, technical or organisational reason entailing changes in the work-force of either the transferor or the transferee before or after the relevant transfer'. Such dismissals are fair provided they pass the statutory test of reasonableness. It is now clear that, if the employer does successfully establish the ETO defence, an employee can claim a redundancy payment if redundancy was the reason for the transfer: *Gorictree Ltd v Jenkinson* [1984].

The scope of the ETO defence was considered by the Court of Appeal in *Berriman v Delabole Slate Ltd* [1985]. Here, it was held that, in order to come within reg 7(3), the employer must show that the change in the workforce is part of the economic, technical or organisational reason for dismissal. It must be an objective of the employer's plan to achieve changes in the workforce, not just a possible consequence of the plan. So, where an employee resigned, following a transfer, because the transferee employer proposed to remove his guaranteed weekly wage so as to bring his pay into line with the transferee's existing workforce, the reason behind the plan was to produce uniform terms and conditions and was not in any way intended to reduce the number of the workforce.

Exclusions

The regulations do not cover rights and liabilities relating to the provision of occupational pension schemes, which relate to benefits for old age, invalidity or survivors (reg 10 and see *Walden Engineering Co Ltd v Warrener* [1993]). Criminal liabilities are not transferred.

Note that the Court of Justice has narrowed this exception in *Beckmann v Dynamco Whicheloe Macfarlane Ltd* [2002].

The regulations apply only to the transfer of an undertaking from one legal person to another. Examples include the transfer of leases and franchises and the outsourcing of services (subject to *Suzen* [1997]). They do not apply to the transfer of shares in a company which carries on the undertaking: see *Brookes and Others v Borough Care Services and CLS Care Services Ltd* [1998].

In *Katsikas v Konstantidis* [1993], the Court of Justice held that an employee could not be transferred to the employment of a new employer without his/her consent. As a result, s 33(4) of the Trade Union Reform and Employment Rights Act 1993 has amended reg 5 so as to provide that the transfer of the contract of employment will not occur if the employee informs the transferor/transferee that he/she objects to becoming employed by the transferee. In that event, the transfer will terminate the employee's contract of employment with the transferor, but he/she will not be treated for any purpose as having been dismissed by the transferor. This exception might be of importance in the context of restrictive/garden leave covenants, where continuing obligations will dissolve.

DUTY TO CONSULT

There exists a duty on employers to consult with workers over any planned redundancies or transfer of undertakings following the EU Directive on Collective Dismissals (75/129/EEC) as amended by (98/59/EC). These provisions are contained in TULR(C)A ss 188–198 and for transfers TUPE 2006 regs 13–16.

The EAT has also stated that there is a duty on the employer to consult over the REASON for making the redundancies in the first place. This new decision replaces the previous authorities to the contrary (*UK Coal Mining Ltd v NUM* [2008]). However, the EAT in *Amicus v Glasgow City Council* [2008] held a transferee has no obligation under TUPE 2006 to consult with employee representatives after the transfer on changes which it envisages making in relation to those staff inherited.

The employer has to consult 'appropriate representatives' in the workplace who may be trades union or employee representatives (who the employer may have to elect), following the Court of Justice's decision in *EC Commission v UK* [1994].

In terms of a redundancy, the Court of Justice held that this means the intention of the employer to terminate the contracts rather than the actual termination (*Junk v Kuhnel* [2005]). Therefore the consultation should take place before the notice of dismissals are sent to the employees.

- In the case of between 20 and 99 employees to be made redundant, the minimum consultation period is a period of 30 days before the first dismissal.

- In the case of 100 or more employees the period is 90 days before the first dismissal (TULRCA, s 188).

With regards to collective redundancies, the Court of Appeal in the *United States of America v Nolan* [2010] recently referred a question to the Court of Justice regarding when an employer's duty to consult arises. In the case, a decision was made in March 2006 to close a US army base. The workforce was informed of the closure on 24th April and a consultation process began on 5th June. The issue requiring clarification is that s 188 TULR(C)A 1992 requires consultation to begin when the employer is 'proposing' redundancies, however the EU law (the Collective Redundancies Directive 98/59/EC) requires consultation when the employer is 'contemplating' redundancies. There is also conflicting case law between the broader UK-interpretation (as established in the EAT in *UK Coal Mining Ltd v NUM* [2008]) and the narrower application of the Court of Justice in *Akavan Erityisalojen Keskusliitto Alek RY and others v Fujitsu Siemens Computers OY* [2009]. This is an important area of law and the outcome from the Court of Justice will have significant implications for employers and unions.

In the case of transfers TUPE does not identify any minimum consultation periods, but consultation must take place. The transferor and the transferee both have the obligation to provide information to the appropriate representatives of the employees affected.

In both redundancy and transfer of undertakings, there exists a defence for an employer where special circumstances exist that make it not reasonably practicable for the employer to comply (TULRCA, s 188(7) and TUPE reg 15(2)). A development, of particular significance to those in the construction industry, is *Shanahan Engineering v Unite the Union* [2010] where the EAT held that even in situations where it was not reasonably practicable to comply with the 30-day consultation period, this did not relieve the employer of its consultation requirements under s 188(2)(4) TULR(C)A 1992. Here, a main contractor ordered a sub-contractor to stop work (which was allowed under the agreement) resulting in a required immediate reduction in the workforce. It was considered that the employer could have consulted over (an available) 2–3 day period, and as this was not complied with, protective awards were ordered.

> ### ◗ CLARKS OF HOVE LTD v BAKERS' UNION [1978]
>
> Here the employer summarily dismissed 368 of 380 employees on the day the company ceased trading and did so without consultation. The company had been in financial difficulties for several of the preceding months and had hoped to trade out of its position, but this was to no avail.
>
> The employer attempted to rely on the special circumstances defence but the Court of Appeal rejected the plea. Financial difficulties was not a 'special' circumstance in this case to warrant not following the consultation requirements. The Court continued that if there was some sudden or unforeseeable reason for the insolvency (such as a disaster of some kind) then this may establish the defence.

In the event that there has been a failure to consult over the proposed transfer, the transferor and the transferee will be held jointly and severally liable for this failure (reg 15(9)).

The claim is made by the employee or trades union representative (if there is none then the employees themselves make the claim) although the compensation is awarded to the employees who were not consulted (TULRCA, s 189).

In *Susie Radin Ltd v GMB* [2004] the Court of Appeal held that the protected award granted should not be to compensate the employees for their loss but rather to deter future employers from failing to comply with the law (confirmed in *Sweetin v Coral Racing* [2006]). The award is to reflect the seriousness of the employer's disregard for the law (TULRCA, s 189 and TUPE, reg 16(3)). However, in *Todd v Care Concern GB Ltd* [2010] the EAT distinguished *Susie Radin*. An award of 13-weeks' pay for an employer's failure to inform and consult should not be the starting point where the employer has tried to do something to comply with the statute. The 13-week starting point should only be used where there has been a complete failure to engage with the consultation process.

You should now be confident that you would be able to tick all the boxes on the checklist at the beginning of this chapter. To check your knowledge of Redundancy payments why not visit the companion website and take the Multiple Choice Question test. Check your understanding of the terms and vocabulary used in this chapter with the flashcard glossary.

7

Collective labour relations

Employees involved in industrial action have limited rights to claim for unfair dismissal	
Pay may be lawfully withheld from striking workers	
Industrial action may constitute a breach of contract enabling an employer to dismiss without notice and/or seek damages	
Trades unions are subject to claims for committing economic torts such as inducement to breach a contract and intimidation of workers	
Immunities from prosecution exist when acting in 'contemplation or furtherance of a trade dispute' (the golden formula). This protects against the tort of interference with contract	
The immunity is lost in situations contrary to good faith (such as secondary actions etc)	
Lawful ballots are required of trades union members before industrial action may be lawfully taken and strict rules apply to their administration	
Industrial action can involve civil and criminal liabilities	

INDUSTRIAL ACTION

In the UK, there is no positive right to strike. Indeed in *Metrobus v Unite the Union* [2010], Maurice LJ remarked 'The right to strike has never been much more than a slogan or a legal metaphor'. Rather than a positive right to strike, there is merely a system of immunities from liability which offer a limited shield of protection to trade unions and strike organisers. This shield, always vulnerable to attack by an unsympathetic judiciary, has been weakened still further by the changes introduced by the governments since 1980. Moreover, those workers who take strike or other industrial action may have some or all of their pay 'docked' and incur the risk of dismissal, with a limited right to challenge its fairness before an employment tribunal.

The changes to collective labour law introduced during the 1980s was put together in one Act of Parliament: the Trade Union and Labour Relations (Consolidation) Act (TULR(C)A) 1992. The relevant provisions of that Act are referred to below.

SANCTIONS AGAINST INDIVIDUAL STRIKERS

DISMISSAL: LIMITED RIGHT TO CLAIM UNFAIR DISMISSAL FOR THOSE TAKING INDUSTRIAL ACTION

See ss 237 and 238 of TULR(C)A 1992, as amended by the Employment Relations Act 1999.

Leading cases

The leading decisions with regard to unfair dismissal claims where industrial action has been taken are:

▓ *Faust v Power Packing Casemakers Ltd* [1983];

▓ *P&O European Ferries (Dover) Ltd v Byrne* [1989];

▓ *Coates v Modern Methods and Materials Ltd* [1982].

Dismissal of unofficial strikers is automatically fair, or, better put, the tribunal has no jurisdiction to hear the case. The same is true of official strikers unless the employers selectively re-engage or selectively dismiss some of the strikers within three months of the start of the action or dismiss any strikers within eight weeks (or after that period if the employers have taken no steps to resolve the dispute).

Dismissal of an employee who was, or intended to join, a trade union, or has taken part in activities of a trade union at an appropriate time is automatically unfair (the one-year qualification is not necessary – TULR(C)A, s 154).

POSSIBLE LOSS OF REDUNDANCY PAYMENTS
See ss 140(1) and (2) of the Employment Rights Act (ERA) 1996, which deal with misconduct. A strike is misconduct.

SUING FOR BREACH OF CONTRACT

> ▶ NATIONAL COAL BOARD v GALLEY [1958]

> The case involved an agreement between the company and a trade union that established new methods of working. This affected the claimant in that he was to work five days per week and reasonable overtime if required.

> The employee refused to work on Saturdays both before the agreement and after it. The employer claimed against the employee for losses, but it was held that whilst the employer could claim against the employee as the agreement had become part of the contract, the claim was limited to the cost of a substitute rather than loss of output.

DEDUCTIONS FROM WAGES OF THOSE TAKING INDUSTRIAL ACTION
The House of Lords' decision in *Miles v Wakefield Metropolitan District Council* [1987] upholds the principle of 'no work, no pay' as the basis for the mutual obligations between employer and employee.

See *Wiluszynski v Tower Hamlets LBC* [1989] (an employer who refuses to accept partial performance of an employee's contractual obligations can withhold all wages payable during the period of the industrial action); see also *British Telecommunications plc v Ticehurst* [1992].

> ▶ WILUSZYNSKI v TOWER HAMLETS LBC [1989]

An employee followed a request from his trade union to refuse to carry out certain duties.

The employer treated the actions of the employee as a breach of contract and withheld wages unless the employee performed all of his contractual duties. He continued to work in the same manner and subsequently brought an action to recover the proportion of work that he had completed (under substantial performance of contract).

The action failed as, although the employers benefited from the work that was performed, the employer did not direct him in the work, or accept the work undertaken.

LEGAL ACTION AGAINST THE TRADE UNION AND STRIKE ORGANISERS
A three stage framework of analysis.

Stage 1
Does the industrial action give rise to civil liability at common law?

Stage 2
If so, is there an immunity from liability provided by s 219 of TULR(C)A 1992?

Stage 3
If so, has that immunity now been removed by virtue of the changes introduced by the Employment Acts of 1980, 1982, 1988 and 1990; the Trade Union Act 1984; Trade Union Reform and Employment Rights Act (TURERA) 1993, and now contained within TULR(C)A?

STAGE 1: CIVIL LIABILITIES FOR INDUSTRIAL ACTION

INDUSTRIAL ACTION AND HOW IT AFFECTS THE CONTRACT OF EMPLOYMENT
The contract of employment is not suspended during a strike. The traditionally accepted view is that a strike is a breach of contract, that is, a breach of the

obligation on the part of the employee to be ready and willing to work. This is so even if strike notice has been given: this is merely notice of impending breach.

Most other forms of industrial action short of a strike also amount to contractual breaches. If workers 'boycott' (refuse to carry out) certain work, they are in breach for refusing to comply with a reasonable order. A 'go slow' or 'work to rule' probably breaks an implied term not to frustrate the commercial objectives of the business (see *Secretary of State for Employment v ASLEF (No 2)* [1972]).

▶ SECRETARY OF STATE FOR EMPLOYMENT v ASLEF (NO 2) [1972]

The case involved an instruction from the ASLEF trade union to its members to take part in industrial action by performing a 'work to rule'.

This resulted in the exact instructions for individuals outlined in the works' handbook being followed. This included refusing overtime and rest-day working. The action was aimed at disrupting the employer's work rather than protecting the workers' health and safety.

The Court of Appeal held that even by following the contract, the employees had breached their obligation to serve their employer faithfully.

An overtime ban will also certainly amount to breach of contract if the employer is entitled under the contract to demand overtime, but not necessarily if overtime is voluntary on the part of the employee (see *Faust v Power Packing Casemakers Ltd* [1983]).

As we have seen, where the industrial action does constitute breach, the employer may summarily dismiss or sue for damages. But, in relation to strike organisers, the true significance of a finding of breach is that it constitutes the 'unlawful means' element necessary in certain economic torts (see below).

THE ECONOMIC TORTS

It is possible to place the torts relevant to industrial action under four broad headings:

- inducement of breach of contract;

- interference with contract, trade or business;

- intimidation;

- conspiracy.

Inducement of breach of contract

This is the main economic tort and derives from *Lumley v Gye* [1853]. The inducement may take one of two forms: direct or indirect. There is a possible defence of justification.

Direct inducement

Direct inducement occurs where the defendant induces a third party to break an existing contract which the third party has with the claimant, who thereby suffers loss. It may help to conceptualise this and other torts if the position is expressed in diagrammatic form.

Inducement		*Breach of employment contract*	
Ann	→	**Brenda** →	**Capital plc**
(Union official)		(Employee)	(Employer)

In the above example, Brenda is employed by Capital plc. Ann, a trade union officer, instructs her to strike. Ann is directly inducing Brenda to break her contract with Capital and is, therefore, committing a tort.

The necessary elements of this form of the tort are:

- knowledge of the contract;

- intention to cause its breach;

- evidence of an inducement;

- actual breach.

Unlawful means are not needed.

Note also that this form of the tort can be committed where a union puts pressure directly on one of the employer's suppliers to cease delivery of vital supplies, thereby inducing breach of a commercial contract. However, boycotting the employer in dispute usually arises as the second form of the tort, that is, indirect inducement.

Indirect inducement

Indirect inducement occurs where the unlawful means are used to render performance of the contract by one of the parties impossible.

| *Breach of employment contract* | | | *Breach of commercial contract* | | |
| Ann | → | Brenda | → | Capital plc | → | Delta plc |

In this example, Delta plc's workers are in dispute with their employer. Capital plc is a supplier of Delta. Brenda is employed by Capital as a lorry driver. Ann, a union official, persuades Brenda not to make deliveries to Delta. Not only has Ann directly induced Brenda to break her contract of employment with Capital, she has also used unlawful means and indirectly induced a breach of commercial contract between Capital and Delta (*DC Thomson v Deakin* [1952]).

Interference with contract, trade or business

Interference may be unlawful even if no breach of contract occurs, for example, by preventing performance in cases where the contract contains a *force majeure* clause exempting a party in breach from liability to pay damages: see the county court judgment in *Falconer v ASLEF and NUR* [1986]. There must be unlawful means, such as breach of statutory duty.

More recently, it would appear that this head of liability is even broader in scope, encompassing any intentional use of unlawful means aimed at interfering with the claimant's trade or business, regardless of the existence or not of a contract: *Merkur Island Shipping Corp v Laughton* [1983].

Intimidation

The tort of intimidation may take the form of compelling a person, by threats of unlawful action, to do some act which causes him loss; or intimidating other persons, by threats of unlawful action, with the intention and effect of causing loss to a third party. Prior to 1964, it was assumed that the tort was confined to threats of physical violence but, in that year, the House of Lords held that threats to break a contract were encompassed by the tort:

▶ ROOKES v BARNARD [1964]

The employee had resigned from membership of a trade union. When he refused to rejoin the trade union, the union's members

> served notice on the employer that unless he was dismissed they would withdraw their labour.
>
> The employee brought an action against the trade union for using unlawful means to induce the employer to terminate his contract and/or conspiring to have him dismissed by threatening the employer with strike action.
>
> The House of Lords agreed.

Lord Reid stated: 'If persons combine to do acts which they know will cause loss to a plaintiff by threat to commit a tort against a third person if he does not comply with their demands, that is using unlawful means to achieve their object.'

Conspiracy

This tort may take two forms:

- conspiracy to commit an unlawful act: a conspiracy to commit a crime or tort is clearly included in this category;

- conspiracy to injure by lawful means.

It is the second form of conspiracy which is the greatest threat to strikers, because it makes it unlawful for two or more people to do something which would have been quite lawful if performed by an individual. A conspiracy to injure is simply an agreement to cause deliberate loss to another without justification. The motives or purposes of the defendants are important. If the predominant purpose is to injure the claimant, the conspiracy is actionable. If, on the other hand, the principal aim is to achieve a legitimate goal, the action is not unlawful, even if, in so doing, the claimant suffers injury. Whilst it took the courts some time to accept trade union objectives as legitimate (see *Quinn v Leathem* [1901]), later decisions adopted a more liberal stance (see *Crofter Hand Woven Harris Tweed Co v Veitch* [1942]). As a result, this form of the tort does not pose the threat it once did to trade union activities.

STAGE 2: THE IMMUNITIES

These are contained in s 219 of TULR(C)A 1992.

INDUCEMENT TO BREACH OF CONTRACT

Under the Trade Disputes Act 1906, the immunity for inducements to breach in contemplation or furtherance of a trade dispute only extended to contracts of employment. This had allowed the courts in the 1960s to find ways of holding trade unionists liable for inducing breaches of commercial contracts: see *JT Stratford v Lindley* [1965].

In the mid-1970s, immunity was extended to cover the breach of 'any' contract. The relevant provision states that an act done by a person in contemplation or furtherance of a trade dispute shall not be actionable in tort on the ground only 'that it induces another person to break a contract or interferes or induces any other person to interfere with its performance': see, now, s 219(1)(a) of TULR(C)A 1992.

As we shall see, however, it is important to view this immunity in the context of subsequent legislative developments. Section 219(1)(a) provides a *prima facie* immunity, but this immunity may be lost in certain instances, namely, by taking unlawful secondary action; engaging in secondary picketing; enforcing trade union membership; or taking 'official' industrial action without first having called a secret ballot.

INTERFERENCE WITH CONTRACT, TRADE OR BUSINESS

Section 219(1)(a) provides an immunity against the tort of interference with contract. It does not, however, offer any explicit protection against the wider 'genus' tort of interference with trade or business by unlawful means. As a result, it is of crucial importance to discover whether an act which is immune by virtue of s 219 (inducement to breach of contract, for example) may nonetheless constitute the 'unlawful means' for the tort of interference with trade or business. Before the passage of the Employment Act 1980, s 13(3) of TULRA 1974 (as amended) stated that, 'for the avoidance of doubt', acts already given immunity could not found the unlawful means element of other torts. When the 1980 statute repealed s 13(3), the legal position became confused. However, it would appear that the correct view is that the repeal of s 13(3) has not changed the position. According to the House of Lords in *Hadmor Productions Ltd v Hamilton* [1982], s 13(3) merely confirmed what was obvious from s 13(1), that is, inducement is 'not actionable'. So, if the unlawful means are immune, no liability can arise in tort.

Intimidation

This immunity is contained in s 219(1)(b) of TULR(C)A 1992, which states that an act done by a person in contemplation or furtherance of a trade dispute shall not be actionable in tort on the ground only:

> ... that it consists of his threatening that a contract (whether one to which he is a party or not) will be broken, or its performance interfered with, or that he will induce another person to break a contract or to interfere with its performance.

Conspiracy

Section 219(2) now provides the immunity against simple conspiracy, which was originally contained in the Trade Disputes Act 1906.

THE TRADE DISPUTE IMMUNITY

In order to gain the protection of the immunities, the individual must be acting *in contemplation or furtherance of a trade dispute*. This is known as the 'golden formula'. For analytical purposes, four questions should be asked in order to determine whether the industrial action qualifies:

- Is it between the correct parties? See below.

- Is there a dispute? Note that there may still be a dispute even if the employer is willing to concede to the demands of the union (s 244(4)). Thus, if an employer ceases to supply another company on receiving a threat of strike action by its workforce if it continues to supply, there is still a dispute.

- Is the subject matter of the dispute wholly or mainly related to one or more of the matters listed in s 244(1)? See below.

- Is the action in contemplation or furtherance of a trade dispute?

A trade dispute must relate wholly or mainly to a matter in s 244(1). These matters include the terms of employment, discipline, membership and non-membership of a union and dismissal.

- A trade dispute must be 'between workers and *their* employers' (emphasis added), not between 'employers and workers', which was the previous position. The Act does not allow trade unions and employers' associations to be regarded as parties to a trade dispute in their own right (cf *NWL v Woods* [1979] and see s 244(1) and (5) of TULR(C)A 1992).

■ Disputes between 'workers and workers' are now omitted from the 'trade dispute' definition. Whilst this means that disputes not involving an employer are unlawful, in practice, it is rare for an employer not to be party to inter-union disputes. A demarcation dispute between unions will usually involve a dispute with an employer regarding terms and conditions of employment.

■ A trade dispute must relate 'wholly or mainly' to terms and conditions of employment and the other matters listed as legitimate in s 244 of TULR(C)A 1992.

■ Since 1982, disputes relating to matters occurring outside the UK are excluded from the immunity, unless the UK workers taking action in further- ance of the dispute are likely to be affected by its outcome in terms of the matters listed in s 244 (see s 244(3)).

Political disputes are not 'trade' disputes. An example is a strike against the Government's economic policy (see *Mercury Communications Ltd v Scott-Garner* [1983]).

In contemplation or furtherance

In *Express Newspapers Ltd v McShane* [1980], the main thrust of the decision was that, if a person taking the action honestly believed that it would further the trade dispute, then this is all that matters: there is no room for an objective test: see also *Duport Steels Ltd v Sirs* [1980]. Acts are not done within the golden formula once the dispute is at an end.

STAGE 3: REMOVAL OF THE IMMUNITIES

The scope of the immunities has been restricted by the legislation of the 1980s: the Employment Acts of 1980, 1982, 1988 and 1990; and the Trade Union Act 1984. In this section, we examine the restriction of secondary action; the provi- sions removing immunity in respect of actions aimed at enforcing the closed shop or trade union recognition on an employer; the loss of immunity for unlawful picketing; the requirements for secret ballots before industrial action; and industrial action taken in support of dismissed 'unofficial strikers'.

STATUTORY CONTROL OF SECONDARY ACTION

Secondary action is not considered lawful action, and will not be protected by the 'golden formula'. The main exception to this is the situation detailed in the indirect form of the tort of inducement to breach of contract.

Section 224(4) seeks to limit any attempt to extend the notion of the primary employer. It states that an employer is not to be regarded as party to a dispute between another employer and its workers. This would appear to confirm the thinking of the House of Lords in *Dimbleby & Sons Ltd v National Union of Journalists* [1984] that an employer, even though associated with the employer involved in the primary dispute, was not to be regarded as a party to that dispute.

The other issue of secondary action concerns picketing: the basic immunity of s 219 only applies if the picket is acting lawfully within s 220, of which the main requirement is that workers may only picket their own place of work. Even if the workers do picket their own place of work, their actions may still amount to secondary action because they may induce a breach of the contracts of employment of the employees of other employers.

UNLAWFUL PICKETING

Unlawful picketing, such as picketing a place other than one's own place of work, will not attract immunity under s 219: see s 219(3) of TULR(C)A 1992.

ENFORCING UNION MEMBERSHIP

The Employment Act 1988 further curbed the closed shop. Section 10 removed the immunities contained in s 13 of TULRA 1974 (as amended) from primary industrial action where the reason, or one of the reasons, for the action is that the employer is employing, has employed or might employ a person who is not a member of a trade union or that the employer is failing, has failed or might fail to discriminate against such a person. Section 11 made it unfair for an employer to dismiss an employee or to subject him/her to a detriment on the ground of the employee's non-membership of a union or particular union. In both of the situations covered by ss 10 and 11, the fact that the closed shop has been approved in a ballot is irrelevant: s 222 of TULR(C)A 1992.

Section 14 of the Employment Act 1982 withdrew the immunity where the reason for the industrial action is to compel another employer to 'recognise, negotiate or consult' one or more trade unions or to force the employer to discriminate in contract or tendering on the ground of union membership or non-membership in the contracting or tendering concern: see, now, s 225 of TULR(C)A 1992.

SECRET BALLOTS BEFORE INDUSTRIAL ACTION
See ss 226–35 of TULR(C)A 1992.

Official industrial action will only attract the immunity offered by s 219 of TULR(C)A 1992 if the majority of union members likely to be called upon to take industrial action has supported that action in a properly conducted ballot. There are stringent rules as to when a ballot is so conducted. For example, there must be an independent scrutineer. The requirements for a lawful ballot and the ways in which a union can be held to be vicariously responsible for industrial action underwent considerable additions and modifications as a result of the Employment Acts of 1988 and 1990. To supplement these requirements, a Code of Practice on Trade Union Ballots on Industrial Action was published in September 2000 to take account of changes introduced by the Employment Relations Act 1999. Breach of the Code does not, of itself, give rise to civil or criminal liability, but courts and tribunals must, where relevant, take it into account as evidence of good industrial relations practice. Some guidance through the complexities of the law in this area will now be offered.

When is a ballot required?
A ballot is only required in respect of an 'act done by a trade union'. An act is taken to have been authorised (beforehand) or endorsed (afterwards) by a trade union if it was done, authorised or endorsed by:

- any person who is empowered by the rules so to do;

- the principal executive committee or the president; or

- any other committee of the union or any official of the union (whether employed by it or not).

See s 20(2) of TULR(C)A 1992.

A union may repudiate the purported authorisation or endorsement by the third group, viz, other committees and officials, but can never repudiate the actions of the principal executive committee, president, general secretary or those acting under the rules. The requirements for an effective repudiation are far more stringent and complicated as a result of changes introduced by the Employment Act 1990. To escape liability, the action must be repudiated by the principal executive committee, president or general secretary as soon as reasonably practicable. Furthermore:

■ written notice of the repudiation must be given to the committee or official in question without delay; and

■ the union 'must do its best' to give individual written notice of the fact and date of repudiation, without delay:

■ to every member of the union who the union has reason to believe is taking part, or might otherwise take part, in industrial action as a result of the act; and

■ to the employer of every such member (see, now, s 21(2) of TULR(C)A 1992).

Should these requirements not be complied with, the repudiation will be treated as ineffective. In addition, there is no repudiation if the principal executive committee, president or general secretary subsequently 'behaves in a manner which is inconsistent with the purported repudiation'.

At this stage, it is important to emphasise the fundamental point that, whilst a properly conducted ballot is vital to maintain the protection of the immunities for any action authorised or endorsed by the union, a lawful ballot will not *per se* accord immunity to the action if it is unlawful for other reasons, for example, secondary action or action to enforce the closed shop.

BALLOT REQUIREMENTS
Official industrial action will only attract immunity if the following conditions are met.

Separate ballots for each workplace
The requirement for separate ballots (ss 228(1) and 228A of TULR(C)A 1992 is subject to the following major exceptions:

■ where the union reasonably believed that all the members had the same workplace;

■ where there is some factor:

- which relates to the terms, conditions or occupational description of each member entitled to vote;
- which that member has in common with some or all members of the union entitled to vote.

This allows a trade union to hold a single aggregated ballot covering members from different places of work if all belong to a complete bargaining unit, for example, all electricians or all members employed by a particular employer. If you can make sense of this highly convoluted provision, you will also note that there does not have to be a factor which is common to all voters. There can be several factors, each of which is common to some, for example, all skilled and semi-skilled grades, all part-time workers and electricians. The union must ballot all its members who possess the same relevant factor. So, for example, if it wishes to conduct a ballot of part-time employees employed by a particular employer, it cannot ballot only those part-time employees at workplace A, excluding part-time employees at workplace B.

Ballot papers

The ballot paper must ask either whether the voter is prepared to take part or continue to take part in a strike, or whether the voter is prepared to take part or continue to take part in action short of a strike, or it may ask both questions separately. The voter must be required to answer 'yes' or 'no' to each question and the questions must not be rolled into one: see *Post Office v Union of Communication Workers* [1990]. A strike is defined as a 'concerted stoppage of work' (s 246 of TULR(C)A 1992).

The ballot paper must also specify the identity of the person or persons authorised to call upon members to take industrial action in the event of a vote in favour. This person need not be authorised under the rules of the union, but he/she must be someone who comes within s 20(2) and (4) of TULR(C)A 1992. Section 20(2) provides that ballot papers must also name an independent scrutineer.

Conduct of the ballot

The ballot must comply with ss 227, 230, 232A and 232B of TULR(C)A 1992, as to equal entitlement to vote, secrecy, non-interference by the union's officials, etc. As a result of s 17 of TURERA 1993, the union now must conduct a postal ballot (see, now, s 230(2) of TULR(C)A)). Section 227(1) provides that all those whom the union might reasonably believe will be induced to take part, or to continue to take part, in the strike or industrial action should be entitled to vote. Section 232A provides that that requirement is not satisfied where a trade union member who is called out on strike 'was denied entitlement to vote in a ballot' (see *RJB Mining (UK) Ltd v National Union of Mineworkers* [1997]). Section 230(3) relates to the opportunity to vote and provides that, 'so far as is reasonably practicable, every person who is entitled to vote in the ballot must [be given an opportunity to do so]' (*British Railways Board v NUR* [1989]). Voting must be carried out by marking a paper (s 229(1)).

TIMING OF THE INDUSTRIAL ACTION

The normal rule is that the action must be called within four weeks, beginning with the date of the ballot (s 234(1)). Notice of separate continuous and discontinuous industrial action can be provided in one single document (hence ensuring clarity where separate documents for each action could generate confusion: see *Milford Haven Port Authority v UNITE* [2010]). By the Employment Relations Act 1999, that period may be extended to eight weeks if the union and management agree. Under s 234(2) of TULR(C)A 1992, a union may now apply for an extension of time to allow for the period during which they were prohibited by a court injunction from calling the action. An application has to be made 'forthwith upon the prohibition ceasing to have effect' and no application may be made after the end of the period of eight weeks, beginning with the date of the ballot.

The ballot paper must identify the person or persons authorised to call for industrial action (see above) and, indeed, industrial action will only be regarded as having the support of the ballot if called by this 'specified person' (s 233(1)). Finally, there must be no authorisation or endorsement of the action before the date of the ballot.

TURERA 1993 (as amended by the Employment Relations Act 1999) introduced the following additional requirements:

- Once a ballot has produced a majority in favour of (continuing with) industrial action, a union is required to give the employer seven days' written notice of any industrial action to which the ballot relates. The notice has to contain information which enables the employers to make plans, and identify on what specific date the industrial action will begin.

▓ Where a union proposes to call for intermittent action, such as a series of one-day strikes, it is required to give at least seven days' notice of each day or other separate period of industrial action.

▓ Moreover, if the union suspends or withdraws its support for the action, further notice is required before any subsequent call to resume the action (see, now, s 234A of TULR(C)A 1992).

TURERA 1993 also gave employers the right to receive the following information:

▓ notice of intent to hold the ballot, with details of which workers will be entitled to vote, and of the voting procedure to be adopted in respect of those workers;

▓ a sample copy of the ballot paper, to enable the employer to know which questions will be asked and what other information will appear on the ballot paper; and

▓ the same details of the result as the law requires to be given to the union's members, and a copy of the report of the independent scrutineer for the ballot.

See, now, ss 226A, 231A and 231B of TULR(C)A 1992.

MEMBERS' STATUTORY RIGHT TO PREVENT UNBALLOTED ACTION

Whilst the failure to hold a ballot will result in the loss of immunities the Employment Act 1988 created an additional legal consequence. Where a trade union authorises or endorses 'industrial action' without first holding a ballot, one of its members who has been, or is likely to be, induced to take action may apply to the High Court for an order requiring the union to withdraw the authorisation or reverse the effect of its authorisation or endorsement: see, now, s 62 of TULR(C)A 1992.

INDUSTRIAL ACTION IN SUPPORT OF DISMISSED 'UNOFFICIAL STRIKERS'

The Employment Act 1990 removed the limited unfair dismissal protection to 'unofficial' strikers (see, now, s 237 of TULR(C)A 1992). In order to strengthen the employer's position in such a situation, the 1990 Act removed the statutory immunity from any industrial action if 'the reason, or one of the reasons, for doing it is the fact or belief' that an employer has selectively dismissed one or more of the employees who were taking unofficial action (see, now, s 223 of TULR(C)A 1992).

CIVIL REMEDIES AND ENFORCEMENT

THE CITIZEN'S RIGHT OF ACTION

Any individual may apply to the High Court if a union or another person has performed an unlawful act to induce a person to take part in unlawful industrial action and that action does, or is likely to, prevent or reduce the quality of goods or services supplied to him (s 235A of TULR(C)A 1992). The court order instructs the defendant to desist.

INJUNCTIONS

An injunction is an order requiring the defendant to cease a particular course of action (a negative injunction) or, in its mandatory form, requiring the defendant to *do* something. The most frequent form of order in industrial disputes is the interim injunction, requiring the organisers to call off the industrial action pending full trial of the action. The award of such an injunction may break the strike.

It used to be the case that, in order to be granted interim relief, the claimant had to establish a *prima facie* case. However, in *American Cyanamid Co v Ethicon Ltd* [1975] (a case involving patents law), the House of Lords substituted a less arduous test: namely, whether there is 'a serious issue' to be tried.

Additionally, the claimant must show that the defendant's conduct is causing him irreparable harm: harm that cannot be remedied by a subsequent award of damages (the 'status quo' concept).

Finally, the claimant must convince the court that the harm being suffered by him is greater than will be incurred by the defendants if they are ordered to cease their activities pending full trial (the 'balance of convenience' test).

The application of these tests generally produced a favourable result for the claimant employer. In determining the status quo and balance of convenience tests, it is easy to quantify the economic loss to an employer as a result of a strike, but it is far more difficult to assess the enormous damage that can be done to the union's bargaining position if the injunction is granted. This, together with the fact that interim relief can be obtained on affidavit evidence at very short notice and without the defendants even having an opportunity to answer the complaint, meant that the process was very much tilted in favour of management. The Court of Appeal, in *The National Union of Rail, Maritime & Transport Workers v Serco Limited (& others)* [2011], where the Court overturned injunctions against strikes involving the appellant unions, provided guidance for unions on how to avoid the 'traps and hurdles' (per Lady Smith) they faced when balloting members on industrial action. As such, this judgment should make obtaining interim injunctions more difficult. This is particularly so in relation to s 232B of TULR(C)A 1992 and accidental ballot errors.

Section 221 of TULR(C)A 1992 contains two provisions which seek to redress the imbalance:

■ Section 221(1) requires reasonable steps to be taken to give notice of the application and an opportunity to be heard for a party likely to put forward a trade dispute defence

■ Section 221(2) provides that, where a party against whom an interim injunction is sought claims that he acted in contemplation or furtherance of a trade dispute, the court shall have regard to the likelihood of that party succeeding in establishing a trade dispute defence. This was an attempt to mitigate the effects of *Cyanamid* in labour injunction cases.

See Lord Diplock's change of attitude between *NWL v Woods* [1979] and *Dimbleby & Sons Ltd v National Union of Journalists* [1984].

Recently, the High Court and Court of Appeal have considered the use of interim injunctions and their effects on the parties. In *British Airways plc v Unite the Union* [2010] the High Court had granted injunctions against planned strike action by British Airways' cabin crew due to breaches of balloting rules (s 231 of TULR(C)A 1992. Despite arguments that the strict rules of the TULR(C)A 1992 breached the Human Rights Act 1998 and Article 11 of the European Convention on Human Rights, the High Court considered it was bound by the ruling in *Metrobus Ltd v Unite the Union* [2009] and could not declare the Act a breach of the Human Rights Act 1998. However, in the High Court Cox J did

145

remark: 'Sooner or later, the extent to which the current statutory regime is in compliance with those international obligations and with relevant international jurisprudence will fall to be carefully reconsidered'.

Breach of an injunction is a contempt of court. A fine for contempt is unlimited; it is not subject to the caps detailed in the next section.

DAMAGES

Probably the most significant change in the structure of labour law during the 1980s was the Employment Act 1982. This made it possible to sue a trade union for unlawful industrial action. In doing this, the Act 'broke the mould' of British labour law, which had been used, but for the brief interlude of the Industrial Relations Act 1971, since 1906.

A union will be held vicariously liable for the unlawful industrial action of its membership where such action was authorised or endorsed by those identified in s 20(2) of TULR(C)A 1992.

Limits on damages awarded against trade unions in actions in tort

Section 22 of TULR(C)A 1992 places limits on the amounts which can be awarded against trade unions in actions brought against them where they have authorised or endorsed unlawful industrial action. The limits, which depend on the size of the trade union, are:

- £10,000 for unions with fewer than 5,000 members;

- £50,000 for unions between 5,000 and fewer than 25,000 members;

- £125,000 for unions with more than 25,000 but fewer than 100,000 members;

- £250,000 if the union has 100,000 or more members.

These limits apply in 'any proceedings in tort brought against a trade union'. The effect of this phrase is that, where a union is sued by various claimants (for example, the employer in dispute, customers, suppliers, etc) for the damages caused to them by the unlawful action, then the maximum will be applied to them separately.

PICKETING

Civil actions and criminal prosecutions may arise as a result of picketing.

THE FREEDOM TO PICKET

As with strike action, English law provides no right to picket. Instead, it offers an extremely limited immunity from civil and criminal liability. This is now contained in s 220 of TULR(C)A 1992. Section 220(1)(a) states that:

> It shall be lawful for a person in contemplation or furtherance of a trade dispute to attend:
>
> (a) at or near his own place of work; or
> (b) if he is an official of a trade union, at or near the place of work of a member of that union whom he is accompanying and whom he represents, for the purposes only of communicating information or peacefully persuading any person to work or abstain from working.

Picketing will only receive the protection of the immunities if the pickets are attending at or near their own workplace. There is no right to stop vehicles. So called 'secondary picketing' was rendered unlawful by the Employment Act 1980. Flying pickets are also unlawful. There is no statutory definition of 'place of work'. However, the Department for Business, Innovation and Skills' Code of Practice on Picketing, to accompany the amendments to the Employment Act 1980, offers the following guidance:

> The law does not enable a picket to attend lawfully at an entrance to, or exit from, any place of work other than his own. This applies even, for example, if those working at the other place of work are employed by the same employer or are covered by the same collective bargaining arrangements as the picket [para 18].

See *Rayware Ltd v TGWU* [1989].

The Act provides three exceptions to the 'own place of work' requirement:

- If workers normally work at more than one place (mobile workers) or if it is impractical to picket their place of work (for example, an oil rig), the section allows them to picket the place where their work is administered by the employer (s 220(2)).

■ Workers who are dismissed during the dispute in question are permitted to picket their former place of work (s 220(3)).

■ As will be seen from s 220(1)(b), a trade union official may attend at any place of work, provided that:

● he/she is accompanying a member or members of his/her trade union who are picketing at their own place of work; and
● he/she personally represents those members within the trade union. An official – whether lay or full time – is regarded, for this purpose, as representing only those members he/she has been specifically appointed or elected to represent. So, it is lawful for a regional official to attend a picket at any place within that region, whereas a shop steward can only picket the workplace of the work group that he/she represents (see s 220(4)).

CIVIL LIABILITIES

THE ECONOMIC TORTS

Without the protection of the immunities, picketing will generally result in an economic tort being committed. If workers assemble at the entrance to a workplace and attempt to persuade other employees not to work, the pickets could be liable for inducing a breach of contracts of employment. However, provided the picketing is lawful within s 220, the general immunity provided by s 219, in respect of tortious liability, applies: see s 219(3).

PRIVATE NUISANCE

Private nuisance is an unlawful interference with an individual's use or enjoyment or use of his land. Unreasonable interference with that right by, for example, blocking an access route to the employer's property, may give rise to a cause of action. So, even though the pickets stand outside the employer's premises, they may be liable for the tort of private nuisance.

Picketing which exceeds the bounds of peacefully obtaining or communicating information may involve liability for private nuisance. However, there is still doubt as to whether peaceful picketing itself amounts to a nuisance when not protected by the 'golden formula': see *Lyons v Wilkins* [1896]; *Mersey Dock and Harbour Co Ltd v Verrinder* [1982]; cf *Ward Lock & Co v Operative Printers' Assistants' Society* [1906]; *Hubbard v Pitt* [1975] (*per* Lord Denning MR).

▶ MERSEY DOCK AND HARBOUR CO LTD v VERRINDER [1982]

Here haulage contract work had been reduced with an economic recession and operators using 'cowboy' operators who were under-cutting the established operators.

The Transport and General Workers Union (TGWU) started a process of issuing 'container stamps' to the established operators with the result that only vehicles displaying those stamps would be serviced by Dockers and TGWU members. In 1981 picketing began that affected the Mersey Dock.

An injunction was granted to restrain the picket and the court held that this could constitute a private nuisance due to the intentions of the defendants.

Thomas v NUM (South Wales Area) [1985]

Two important points arise from this decision:

▣ Private nuisance is concerned with interference with the use or enjoyment of land in which the claimant has an interest. In this case, a species of the tort was held to extend to interference with the right to use the highway.

▣ The terms of the injunction granted by the court restricted picketing at the collieries to peacefully communicating and obtaining information in numbers not exceeding six. This number is not a purely arbitrary figure – it comes from the Code of Practice on Picketing which advises that (para 51):

... pickets and their organisers should ensure that, in general, the number of pickets does not exceed six at any entrance to a work-place; frequently, a smaller number will be appropriate.

This would suggest that the judge was using the guidance in the Code to fix the parameters of lawful picketing. If this view is correct, then any picketing numbering more than six will lose the immunity offered by s 220 and will be tortious.

TRESPASS

Section 220 of the Trade Union and Labour Relations (Consolidation) Act 1992

Picketing is lawful where pickets attend 'at or near' their own place of work. To mount a picket on the employer's land without consent will mean that the immunity will be forfeited and that the tort of trespass has been committed: see *British Airports Authority v Ashton* [1983]. Special damage is necessary and only the highway owners may sue.

CRIMINAL LIABILITIES

Whilst it is important to grasp the range of possible civil liabilities which may attach to certain types of picketing, it is the criminal law which is of the greatest practical significance in terms of control of the activity.

OBSTRUCTING A POLICE OFFICER IN THE EXECUTION OF HIS DUTY

If a police officer reasonably apprehends that a breach of the peace is likely to occur, he has the right and duty at common law to take reasonable steps to prevent it. If the officer is obstructed in the exercise of this duty, an offence is committed: s 96(3) of the Police Act 1996. In practice, this gives the police a wide discretion to control picketing. While there must be an objective apprehension that a breach of the peace is a real – as opposed to a remote – possibility, the courts tend to accept the officer's assessment of the situation: see *Piddington v Bates* [1960]; *Moss v McLachlan* [1985].

> ▶ MOSS v McLACHLAN [1985]
>
> The case involved striking miners who were stopped when travelling in a convoy of vehicles on a route towards four collieries in Nottinghamshire.
>
> The police officer in charge informed the men that he had reason to believe they intended to join the demonstrations at these collieries, and would not allow them to continue as he feared there would be a breach of the peace. A group, including the appellants, stopped their vehicles, blocking the road, and attempted to push past the police.

It was held that this action amounted to obstructing the officer in the execution of his duties and the order of the police was lawful.

OBSTRUCTION OF THE HIGHWAY

Section 137 of the Highways Act 1980

Under this provision, it is an offence wilfully to obstruct free passage along a highway without lawful authority or excuse.

Before the offence is established, there must be proof of an unreasonable use of the highway. This is a question of fact and depends upon all the circumstances, including the length of time the obstruction continues, the place where it occurs, its purpose and whether it causes an actual as opposed to a potential obstruction (*Nagy v Weston* [1965]). It would appear that peaceful picketing carried out in the manner envisaged by s 15 of TULR(C)A 1992 and within the numbers advised by the Code will be held to be a reasonable user. If, however, these boundaries are crossed, the offence will be committed; as where pickets stood in front of a vehicle in order to prevent it from entering the employer's premises (*Broome v DPP* [1974]) and walked in a continuous circle at a factory entrance (*Tynan v Balmer* [1967]).

PUBLIC NUISANCE

This offence derives from common law and is committed where members of the public are obstructed in the exercise of rights that are common to all Her Majesty's subjects, including the right of free passage along the public highway. As with the more frequently charged offence under the Highways Act, it is necessary for the prosecution to prove unreasonable use.

Where an individual suffers special damage over and above that suffered by the rest of the public, an action in tort for public nuisance may also be brought.

> ▶ NEWS GROUP NEWSPAPERS LTD v SOCIETY OF GRAPHICAL AND ALLIED TRADES [1986]
>
> The claimants were a group of companies who brought an action seeking injunctions against the defendant trade unions. There had

been unsuccessful negotiations between the parties with the result that the employer's workers went on strike.

These workers were dismissed and the production transferred to new premises at Wapping. The Union organised pickets at both the new and old premises, which involved abusive and threatening behaviour, and some workers being assaulted. The pickets also prevented traffic from passing to and from Wapping and other acts of intimidation and violence were alleged.

The court issued interim injunctions to prevent these acts of public nuisance.

Conspiracy and Protection of Property Act 1875

This Victorian statute made the following acts criminal if they are done 'wrongfully and without legal authority', with a view to compelling any person to do or abstain from doing any act which that person has a legal right to do:

- using violence or intimidating that person or his wife or children or injuring his property;

- persistently following that person about from place to place;

- hiding any tools, clothes or other property owned or used by such other person, or depriving him or hindering him in the use thereof;

- watching or besetting his house, residence or place of work, or the approach to such house, residence or place, or wherever the person happens to be;

- following such a person with two or more other persons, in a disorderly manner, in or through any street or road (see, now, s 241 of TULR(C)A 1992).

This provision was frequently resorted to during the miners' strike of 1984–85. Subsequently the Public Order Act 1986 increased the maximum penalty from three months' imprisonment and a £100 fine to six months' imprisonment and a fine (currently £5,000). The Act also made breach of what is now s 241 an arrestable offence.

One final point on this section concerns the question of whether mass picketing amounts to intimidation. In *Thomas v NUM (South Wales Area)* [1985], Scott J was of the view that not only was mass picketing a common law nuisance, but also that it amounted to intimidation under what is now s 241, even where there was no physical obstruction of those going to work.

Public Order Act 1986

Part I of the Public Order Act contained five new statutory offences which may be of relevance in the context of picketing. Sections 1–3 of the Act contain the offences of rioting, violent disorder and affray and replace the common law offences of riot, rout, unlawful assembly and affray, whose ambit was confused and uncertain. Sections 4 and 5 contain the more minor offences of causing fear or provocation of violence and causing harassment, alarm or distress.

Part II gives the police certain powers to impose conditions upon public processions and assemblies, in addition to their common law powers to take such action as may be necessary to prevent a breach of the peace.

You should now be confident that you would be able to tick all the boxes on the checklist at the beginning of this chapter. To check your knowledge of Collective labour relations why not visit the companion website and take the Multiple Choice Question test. Check your understanding of the terms and vocabulary used in this chapter with the flashcard glossary.

Putting it into practice...

8

Now that you've mastered the basics, you will want to put it all into practice. The Routledge Questions and Answers series provides an ideal opportunity for you to apply your understanding and knowledge of the law and to hone your essay-writing technique.

We've included one exam-style essay question, which replicates the type of question posed in the Routledge Questions and Answers series to give you some essential exam practice. The Q&A includes an answer plan and a fully worked model answer to help you recognise what examiners might look for in your answer.

QUESTION 1

While employment tribunals can provide a quick and efficient remedy for an aggrieved employee, the restrictions placed upon them created problems for employees who wished to sue their employer. Changes made by the Trade Union Reform and Employment Rights Act (TURERA) 1993 eradicated these problems, and provided tribunals with a comprehensive power to protect employees against infringement of all their rights.

Critically evaluate this statement.

> ### Common Pitfalls
>
> It is important to read what the question is asking for. A list of all the changes made by the Act does not answer the question, which asks you to critically evaluate the statement.
>
> You must identify the problems pre-1993. Note the changes made by TURERA and see which problems have been eradicated and which still exist.

Answer Plan

This question falls nearly into two parts: the first part asks about the problems facing employees before the TURERA 1993; the second part asks for a discussion of the changes made by the Act and consideration of whether these changes eradicated the problems identified.

The issues to be considered are:

■ tribunal jurisdiction before the TURERA 1993;

■ limits on the jurisdiction;

■ the problems that such limits caused;

■ other problems caused by restrictions in making tribunal claims;

■ how the jurisdiction was extended in 1994; and

■ whether the present jurisdiction has met the problems identified earlier.

ANSWER

Employment tribunals were established by the Industrial Training Act 1964 with limited jurisdiction. Over the years, however, the jurisdiction was extended until, prior to amendments by the TURERA 1993, tribunals had the jurisdiction to hear almost all individual disputes based on statutory claims. It is important to note, however, that, until the 1994 amendments, tribunals only had jurisdiction to hear statutory claims and, as such, would hear, inter alia, unfair dismissal disputes, redundancy disputes, sex and race discrimination claims, and equal pay claims. Tribunals had no jurisdiction to hear common law claims, which had to be heard by the ordinary courts. In addition, other criticisms have been levelled against tribunals, which jurisdictional changes will not address. These further criticisms will be discussed below.

Perhaps the major problem facing an employee before the changes made by the 1993 Act was the fact that tribunals could not hear common law claims. While on the face of things this did not appear to be a major problem, in fact, an unfair dismissal claim would often also involve a common law claim for damages for breach of contract. While the employee could sue for the unfair dismissal in the tribunal, the damages claim could only be heard by the ordinary courts, thus necessitating the employee taking two actions in different forums in relation to the same act by the employer. For example, in *Treganowan v Robert Knee and Co Ltd* [1975], the applicant was instantly dismissed when the typing pool refused to work with her after she kept discussing details of an affair she was having with a work colleague. The tribunal found that she had been fairly dismissed. It further stated that her conduct did not justify instant dismissal and that she should have received the six weeks' notice she was entitled to by her contract. The tribunal, however, had no jurisdiction to hear the breach of contract claim or award damages for what the tribunal considered to be a breach of contract. To pursue an action for damages, Ms Treganowan had to take action in the county court. Furthermore, if the notice had been considerable and, therefore, the damages had been outside the county court jurisdiction, Ms Treganowan would have had to pursue her claim in the High Court. Breach of contractual notice provisions are obviously not the only breach of contract an employer can commit: many cases arise over breaches of express or implied terms in the contract. The tribunals, until 1994, had no jurisdiction over these claims, leaving the employee to use the ordinary courts.

While there had been much criticism of the jurisdictional limit placed upon the tribunals, the extent of the restrictions came to the fore with the introduction of the Wages Act 1986 (now the Employment Rights Act (ERA) 1996). This was brought in to remedy the deficiencies in the Truck Acts 1831–1940 and provides that there must be a statutory or contractual right to deduct from wages before any such deductions can be made. Section 13(1) of the 1996 Act states that an employer must not make a deduction from the wages of an employee unless the deduction is:

(a) required or authorised by statute; or

(b) required or authorised by a provision in the contract of employment that has been given to the employee or notified to the employee previously in writing; or

(c) agreed to by the employee in writing before the making of the deduction.

Section 14 then contains a list of exceptions to which s 13(1) does not apply. The Act has been widely criticised and, prior to the changes in tribunal jurisdiction, led to a series of cases on interpretation. The major problem was whether the Act applied to given situations. An illegal deduction gave an employment tribunal jurisdiction, normally within three months of the deduction being made. Any other deduction had to be recovered in the ordinary courts. This led to a series of cases defining the terms 'wages' and 'deduction' for the purposes of s 13(1) to see if the tribunals had jurisdiction in certain situations.

Section 27 of the ERA 1996 lists payments that can be regarded as wages. In particular, s 27(1)(a) refers to 'any fee, bonus, commission, holiday pay, or any other emolument referable to his employment, whether payable under his contract or otherwise'. This definition led to a number of cases discussing whether wages in lieu of notice are 'wages' for the purpose of s 13(1) and therefore whether employment tribunals had the jurisdiction to hear complaints about deductions from such payments. In the House of Lords' decision of *Delaney v Staples t/a De Montfort Recruitment* [1992], their Lordships decided that a payment in lieu was damages for a breach of contract. Such a payment did not arise out of the employment but as a result of the termination of employment and as such was not within the definition in s 27, even if the employer had a contractual right to pay wages in lieu. This decision meant that the tribunals could not hear complaints about deductions from such payments. Such complaints could only be heard by the ordinary courts, a situation acknowledged by the House of Lords, which ended with a plea that the jurisdiction of the tribunals be extended to hear breach of contract claims. Further cases have decided that, while *ex gratia* payments are not wages, it depends on the construction of the contract. In *Kent Management Services Ltd v Butterfield* [1992], an ex-employee complained that on his dismissal his employer had refused to pay him commission that was outstanding. The employer argued that the commission was discretionary as a clause attached to the contract said it would not be paid in exceptional circumstances such as bankruptcy. Wood P in the EAT held that, on interpretation, the anticipation of both parties must have been that, in normal circumstances, commission would be paid. As such, it was wages for the purposes of s 27(1)(a) and the tribunal had the jurisdiction to hear the complaint about the deduction.

The *Kent* case demonstrates another problem of interpretation that arises from the Act. How far is a total non-payment a deduction? The Court of Appeal in the *Delaney* case held that a non-payment was a 100 per cent deduction and, as such, tribunals would have the jurisdiction to hear such complaints. The issue was never raised before the House of Lords, so presumably this is still the law. If the jurisdiction of tribunals had been extended at this time, these problems would not have arisen.

While the limits on the tribunal jurisdiction have raised the major criticisms, other problems can also be identified. The first is the time limits that apply to different claims. These are different depending upon the claim brought. For example, an employee must present a claim for unfair dismissal within three months of the effective date of termination, whereas the time limit is six months on a redundancy claim. While different time limits can be confusing, there are further problems in that the tribunal has the discretion to allow a claim out of time if it was not reasonably practicable for a claim to be made within the three-months period (s 111(2) of the ERA 1996). Given that tribunal decisions are not reported, this can lead to a variation in practice in different tribunals, although some guidelines have been laid down by the courts (see, for example, *London International College v Sen* [1993]). Reporting of tribunal decisions would ensure more consistency.

A further problem lies in the fact that an applicant cannot obtain legal aid for a tribunal claim. Given that a large number of applicants are unemployed at the time of pursuing a case in a tribunal, this can be a major setback. In addition, until changes made in 2001 and 2002, a tribunal had limited powers to award costs where the claim was considered to be frivolous or vexatious and could only award costs of up to £500, a power exercised infrequently. In 1997–98 and 1998–99, they were awarded in fewer than 0.5 per cent of cases. Changes made by the Employment Tribunals (Constitution and Rules of Procedure) Regulations 2004 now give a tribunal the power to award costs where a party or a party's representative has acted improperly. Furthermore, a tribunal must consider awarding costs where a party or its representative has acted 'vexatiously, abusively, disruptively or otherwise unreasonably, or the bringing of the proceedings by the party is misconceived' (reg 14). 'Misconceived' includes having no real prospect of success (reg 2). The amount of costs a tribunal can award has increased to £10,000. While this may benefit a claimant, costs may also be awarded against a claimant and thus the effect of these changes may be to deter potential applicants.

Given the amount of legislation in the past few years in the area of employment law, claims are getting much more complicated and often the applicant will need the skills of a lawyer or other experienced representative to present his or her case. The problem may be exacerbated since the proposals introduced by s 20 of the Employment Act 1989 have come into effect. This section gave the Secretary of State power to make regulations for a pre-hearing review procedure, which would allow the tribunal, after such a review, to order one party to pay a deposit before continuing with the case. The initial amount of the deposit was £150, but this was increased to £500 in 2001. Pre-hearing reviews were introduced by the Employment Tribunals (Rules of Procedure) Regulations 1993. Section 38 of the TURERA 1993 gave the Secretary of State power to extend the jurisdiction of the tribunals to cover claims for damages for breach of contract subject to a financial limit. This extension of jurisdiction was introduced by the Employment Tribunals (Extension of Jurisdiction) Order 1994 (now the Employment Tribunals Act 1996). Personal injury claims are, however, still excluded, as are claims for breach of a term requiring the employer to provide accommodation, breach of a term relating to intellectual property, breach of a term imposing an obligation of confidence and breach of a restraint-of-trade covenant.

In addition, the tribunal jurisdiction applies only where there is a termination of the contract (see *Capek v Lincolnshire County Council* [2000]) and is subject to a £25,000 limit. The extended jurisdiction means that the situation in *Treganowan* will not arise again, as the tribunal can now hear both claims as long as the damages claims is within the financial limits set. Furthermore, the problems raised in *Delaney* relating to wages in lieu of notice are also resolved as, even though such payments are damages for breach of contract, the tribunal has jurisdiction to hear complaints in relation to deductions from such payments. As such, the amendments allowed by the TURERA 1993 have met the problems arising from the restricted tribunal jurisdiction in these types of case, and prevented the duplicity of actions, one in the tribunal and one in the ordinary courts, which used to be necessary.

The other problems identified above were not answered by the 1994 Order. In an area of law that has become increasingly complex over the years, legal aid is still unavailable and, now that the proposals of 1989 in relation to pre-hearing reviews have been enacted, this can only further restrict the number of applicants who can claim. In addition, different time limits in respect of different rights and unreported tribunal decisions, particularly when allowing an applicant to present a claim outside the statutory time limit, emphasise the need for legal aid to be available. Furthermore, the restriction as to the type of breach-of-contract claims that the tribunal can hear, plus the fact that the jurisdiction arises only on termination of the contract, lead one to question whether, in practice, the changes made that much difference. While the changes engendered by the 1993 Act are to be welcomed, the lack of other changes will still mean that not all employees have the opportunity to have their cases heard by an industrial jury.